BEING
UP-TO-DATE
for the
REBUILDING
of the
TEMPLE

WITNESS LEE

Living Stream Ministry
Anaheim, California

First Edition, August 2002.

ISBN 0-7363-1947-6

Published by

Living Stream Ministry
2431 W. La Palma Ave., Anaheim, CA 92801 U.S.A.
P. O. Box 2121, Anaheim, CA 92814 U.S.A.

Printed in the United States of America

02 03 04 05 06 07 08 / 10 9 8 7 6 5 4 3 2 1

CONTENTS

PREFACE

This book is a collection of messages given in Chinese by Brother Witness Lee from August through November of 1987 while leading the service of the church in Taipei, Taiwan. These messages were not reviewed by the speaker.

CHAPTER ONE

THE DEFICIENCIES OF TRADITION
AND THE PROSPECTS OF THE NEW SYSTEM

Scripture Reading: Psa. 52:8; Luke 2:25-32, 36-38

RECEIVING THE ETERNAL LIFE,
A NEVER-AGING LIFE, IN REGENERATION

We all like to encourage the young people to learn more, because young people learn everything quickly. However, the older ones should not be discouraged, because there is a verse in the Bible that says, "So that your youth is renewed like the eagle" (Psa. 103:5). Even if we are old, our youth can be renewed, and we can still have the opportunity to learn.

We saved ones are regenerated people. Once we are regenerated, we cannot get old. The life that we received in our regeneration is an eternal life, a never-aging life. This life is different from the life that we received by birth. The life that we received from our parents is not growing daily but dying daily. If we are destined to live until we are ninety years old, then for every year that passes, we must subtract a year from our life, and for every ten years that pass, we must subtract ten years from our life. For example, if we have ninety dollars, every dollar that we spend means that we have one less dollar to spend. Because many of us do not have many years left, we do not want to waste them. This is not merely a feeling but a fact.

The life that we received in our regeneration is not like the gradually declining life we received by birth. The life that we received in our regeneration is a life that grows daily and is an eternal life. One psalmist in the Bible said, "But I, like a flourishing olive tree / In the house of God" (Psa. 52:8). I believe that this psalm was written by an old, even very aged, psalmist. But although he was old, he did not yield to his oldness. Hymn #715 in the Chinese hymnal says, "The withering days of life are seemingly increasing but actually decreasing." This means that man's life is like withering days that are apparently increasing but are actually decreasing. Some Christians who are already over eighty have subtracted more than eighty years from their life and do not have many years left. However, they have the eternal life in them, and this eternal life renews their youth.

Today the reason some of the elderly saints are so lively is that they have the eternal life in them. Although they themselves may not have this feeling, this is the fact. Their youth is being renewed day by day. In particular, we see many elderly saints in the meetings who welcome people with smiles and are full of vigor. What is real in them is manifested outwardly. They have a life in them that is a never-aging life. When this life is expressed in them, it becomes joy, because our Lord is the Lord of joy. There may be nothing in the outward environment to make us joyful, but the Lord who lives in us is our joy. We are joyful when we sing, and we are even more joyful when we testify for the Lord. The more we open our mouths, the more joyful we are. Even by saying "Amen" or "Hallelujah," our faces become glowing, shining, and full of joy.

CHRIST BEING THE CONSOLATION
AND THE SALVATION OF GOD'S PEOPLE

Even though the writer of Psalm 52 may have been aged, he saw himself as a flourishing olive tree that was growing in the house of Jehovah. I hope that all of us elderly saints would have the feeling that although we are aged, we still are flourishing olive trees. Instead of being weakened, as flourishing olive trees we have been planted in the house of Jehovah and are trusting in God's lovingkindness forever and ever.

In the New Testament Luke 2:25 and 36 mention two elderly saints—one brother and one sister. The brother is named Simeon and the sister is named Anna. Verses 25 through 32 are concerning Simeon. Although this passage is short, it mentions the Holy Spirit three times. The first time it says, "The Holy Spirit was upon him" (v. 25). The Holy Spirit was on Simeon. Today we elderly saints are more blessed than Simeon because the Holy Spirit is not only on us but in us. The second time it says, "It had been divinely communicated to him by the Holy Spirit" (v. 26). It was not through a dream or his thoughts but through his receiving the revelation from the Holy Spirit that Simeon knew that he would not see death before he had seen the consolation of God's people. The Lord Jesus was the consolation of God's people. The elderly Simeon not only had the Holy Spirit but also received revelation from the Holy Spirit. The revelation that he received was concerning Christ. We all should be like Simeon who received a revelation from the Holy Spirit that was not related to peace or prosperity but to Christ.

Simeon received a revelation from the Holy Spirit and knew that he would not see death before he had seen the Lord's Christ, who was the consolation of God's people (vv. 25-26). Later, the Holy Spirit moved him to enter the temple because the consolation of Israel, for whom he had been waiting, had arrived. At that time the Lord Jesus was still a little child. Simeon came in the Spirit into the temple, and the parents of Jesus brought Him in. Once he saw the child, he did not hesitate to receive Him into his arms. He blessed God and said, "Now You release Your slave, Master, according to Your word, in peace; for my eyes have seen Your salvation, which You have prepared before the face of all the peoples" (vv. 29-31). In his two short words, the word says that the Lord Jesus was the consolation of God's people, and the other says that the Lord Jesus was God's salvation (vv. 25, 30). He saw that the Lord Jesus was both the consolation of God's people and God's salvation. The revelation and the spiritual feeling that Simeon received were both concerning Christ.

Today many Christians claim that they have received a revelation and have been touched to preach the gospel to certain relatives to save them from hell and perdition. Although we cannot say that this is bad, it is certainly not very high. Simeon received the revelation to see that Christ was the consolation of God's people; he was also moved to receive Christ and said that he had seen God's salvation. This proves that in his old age the elderly Simeon did not care for anything other than Christ. Every day he focused on Christ based upon God's promise. The Old Testament promised again and again that Christ would come, and it hinted that Christ was the consolation of God's people. Moreover, there were clear types showing that Christ was the salvation of God's people. The elderly Simeon must have nearly memorized the entire Old Testament because he knew very well that these promises, hints, and types all referred to Christ.

Simeon was inwardly filled with Christ as the consolation of God's people and God's salvation. It could be said that he was charmed and captured by Christ. Hence, the revelation that he received was Christ, and he was moved with Christ. This is an excellent example for us. However, even though the elderly Simeon was merely in the Old Testament and had not entered the New Testament, he received such a high revelation. He arrived at such a revelation merely by enjoying the grace in the Old Testament. Nevertheless, he is truly a good pattern for us. Today what do we elderly ones think about? If we think about our children, there will be no end to our thinking. Of course, all parents think about their children, but we have to realize that it is not worthwhile to think about our children so much. To do so is to look for trouble. When we think about our children so much, not only are we unable to render them help, but sometimes we may be bound by them or cause them to be bound by us. This is truly pitiful.

After the account concerning Simeon, the Gospel of Luke gives the record of an elderly sister named Anna who loved Christ very much and pursued Christ. Luke 2 mentions these two elderly saints, showing us that they both considered Christ. This is very precious. I want to ask the younger saints what you think about. Do you think about beautiful clothing, good food, and high positions? Most young people think about what to wear and how to adorn themselves whereas most elderly people do not think about these things. Rather, they think about their children. It is truly a blessing for some elderly saints that they do not have children. If you do not have children, you will be unoccupied. A person spends all his money for himself when he is young, but when he is old, he saves every penny for his children. The sisters are especially frugal and thrifty for their children. Hence, it is hard for elderly people to overcome their preoccupation with their children, and it is not easy for young people to overcome their preoccupation with adornment.

The elderly Simeon and Anna were not like this. Their hearts were on Christ. I have eight children, twenty-two grandchildren, and two great-grandchildren. When I am among them, listening to their stories, I really need the Lord to put the helmet of salvation upon me. I would like to tell the elderly people that our children are not our consolation. Only Christ is our consolation and our salvation. The more the elderly people are focused on Christ, the more blessed they will be. If we dream of Christ at night, think about Christ in the morning, talk about Christ all the time, and are full of Christ, we will be blessed.

THE CHANGE IN SYSTEM BEING NOT A CHANGE IN OUTWARD PRACTICE BUT A CHANGE IN OUR LIVING

The churches changed their system of practicing the church life several years ago. This kind of change in system, however, should not be merely a change in outward practice but a change in our living. In the past we elderly people were filled with either our daughters and sons or with our sons-in-law, daughters-in-law, and grandchildren. If we are filled with them, we will have nothing to say when we come to the meeting. Sometimes our body is in the meeting, but our mind is thinking about our children. Even in the Lord's table meeting when we are remembering the Lord, we are still thinking about our children. Apparently we are breaking the bread and drinking the cup, but what we are thinking about and remembering inwardly is not the Lord but our children. What a pitiful situation this is!

Blessed are those who do not have children. When they remember the Lord, they simply remember the Lord. Although some elderly ones who are like this may be lonely, they do not have any anxiety. When they break the bread and drink the cup, they remember the Lord wholeheartedly. Aside from the

Lord they have no one to remember. They are like the psalmist who said, "Whom do I have in heaven but You? / And besides You there is nothing I desire on earth" (Psa. 73:25). The elderly Simeon was like this, simply loving the Lord and looking to the Lord. If we all lived in this kind of condition, we would spontaneously open our mouths to praise the Lord when we come to the meeting. When those who always think about their children in their hearts open their mouths in the meeting, there is a danger that once they open their mouths the content of their speaking will be their children. Matthew 12:34 says, "For out of the abundance of the heart the mouth speaks."

LEARNING FROM SIMEON AND ANNA
TO CONSIDER CHRIST AND SPEAK CHRIST

Simeon not only pointed out that Christ is our consolation and our salvation, but he continued to say in Luke 2:32 that Christ is "a light for revelation to the Gentiles and the glory of Your people Israel." Christ's coming to us is light and glory. If, like Simeon, we think about Christ, speak Christ, and even dream about Christ at night, our change of the system will surely be successful. Our changing the system in these few years is not to change the way of our meetings or merely to change a method. The change in system requires us to dream of Christ, receive a revelation of Christ, and be touched by Christ so that once we open our mouths, we will speak Christ. Christ is our patience, and Christ is our joy. Yesterday what we thought about was Christ, and today what we think about is also Christ. When we go to work, we should be think about Christ, and when we go home to do our laundry and cooking, we should still be thinking about Christ. What we think about day and night should be Christ. I hope that we all would be encouraged to rise up to be a Simeon.

The account concerning Anna shows us more about our experience of Christ. The Gospel of Luke tells us that this elderly sister was "serving God with fastings and petitions night and day" (v. 37b). She not only prayed but also fasted and petitioned. Eventually she saw Christ. Once she saw Christ, she spoke concerning Him to all the people. Verse 38 says, "She came up and returned thanks to God, and spoke concerning Him to all those waiting for the redemption of Jerusalem." Her speaking must have been something remarkable; otherwise, Luke would not have recorded this.

When Anna spoke about Christ, she could not stop. All elderly people, especially sisters, like to talk about their children. Whenever they talk about their children, they cannot stop. They gossip and make critical remarks about people's appearances, and in the end they lose Christ. However, Anna was not like this. She spoke Christ to everyone. I hope that we all, especially the sisters, would exercise not to speak about our children but to speak about Christ. If people ask us how our sons or sons-in-law are doing, we would say, "I thank the Lord that everything is fine. Let us talk about Christ."

Anna not only spoke about Christ, but her prayer was filled with praises of Christ. The main point in considering Simeon and Anna is that if all the elderly brothers were like Simeon and all the elderly sisters were like Anna, when we all came together, we would not be without anything to say. We would also become those who love to meet, because we would realize that it is not very enjoyable to speak merely to our family at home. We would realize our need to be with all the saints and to speak Christ for the building up the Body of Christ.

THE DIFFICULTY AND HARDSHIP
IN CHANGING THE SYSTEM

In our meetings in the past, we always had one who stood on the platform and spoke. Moreover, we have never been trained to speak for the Lord in the meetings. As a result, we do not know how to lead people to speak for the Lord, and the most we can do is to encourage them to give their testimonies in the meetings. If we consider those who are mothers, we will realize that what they worry about is that their children will not know how to speak. It is universally known that if a child does not begin to speak by the time he is a year old, his mother will begin to worry about him and try to make him speak. All mothers know that it is their important task to make their children speak. In the beginning when a child is learning to speak, the more he speaks, the happier his mother is.

When people come to our meetings, even though we do not have a sign saying, "Please remain silent" or "No talking," the form of our meetings is already like a sign, causing those who come to the meetings to not speak. Even though they have Christ within, they do not speak, because everything we do in the meetings—including our singing, reading of the Scriptures, praying, and listening to the messages—already has an invisible arrangement and agenda. Thus, it is hard for people to be free in the meetings.

We deeply understand that changing the system is like changing one's habit and that to do so is not easy. We have been meeting for more than thirty years. In the meetings over these past thirty years, there were some who called hymns, some who prayed, and some who spoke. The messages released in the meetings were rich, so when people came to the meetings, they did not need to function and only needed to wait for those who were taking the lead. This is the habit that has been developed. Now, however, we are suddenly saying that we have to change this system and get rid of the old way. Surely the saints will not be used to such a change.

Owing to the influence from the West, my mother sent me to an English institution in China to study English after I finished elementary school. Later, I was admitted to an American school in China. Everything in the school was American. Even our textbooks had been imported from America. Among all the teachers there was only one who was Chinese. This teacher taught Chinese literature. The rest of the teachers were all American. The students were of many different nationalities. Although we were studying in an American school, none of us dared to wear a suit, because if we wore suits, we would be scolded. At that time if someone were to walk on the street in a suit, people on the street would scold him for conforming to Western fashion. Even though we all learned English quite well, we did not have the boldness to speak English because if we were to speak, we would also be scolded.

After I graduated from school, I worked in a company with

people of seven different nationalities—German, French, British, American, Greek, Norwegian, and Russian. Because I had also studied some foreign languages, I worked among them for seven and a half years. At that time I still wore a long gown every day while walking among them. In 1949 when I began to preach in different places I did not have a suit or a shirt. All I had were long gowns. It was not until a year later when I went to the Philippines that I started to wear suits. Therefore, I know that it is extremely difficult to change one's habit or system.

THE DEFICIENCIES OF THE TRADITIONAL MEETINGS IN THE OLD SYSTEM

Our traditional way of meeting was inherited from Christianity. Although we have been delivered from Christianity, the traditions of Christianity have not been purged from us. In the past, we did not see any other way to meet besides the traditional way. Hence, our meetings followed the tradition of Christianity. On the one hand, the old way of meeting was successful, but on the other hand, it matched our natural man. The older generation always charged the young people not to speak much, regardless of where they went or what the occasion was, because young people easily make mistakes. Therefore, they taught that the less you speak, the fewer mistakes you will make. If you do not speak, you will make no mistakes, but if you speak much, you will make many mistakes. This became a motto for people in general. Thus, when people come to the meetings, they just sit quietly and wait for the preacher to speak a good message for them. This kind of meeting, in which one person speaks and everyone else listens, is very convenient and is welcomed by almost everyone.

During the first few years that I began the work in the United States, we had a twenty to thirty percent increase in number every year. But in the past five years we have had an increase of less than two percent. When I discovered this, it made me very discouraged, and I wanted to find out the reason. So I came back to Taiwan to study the condition in Taiwan, and I found out that even though we were preaching the gospel and baptizing people every year, in the end the total number was still decreasing.

Some people told me that the reasons for the decrease were twofold. They said that the first reason was that many saints from Taipei had moved away because they had remodeled or built new houses outside Taipei and that when these ones moved away, we lost track of their whereabouts. This statement is not completely correct because we did not lose the whereabouts of any of those who moved. They said that the second reason was that more and more younger saints were going to the United States to study. This is surely true, but we cannot say that the number of those who went abroad to study exceeded the number of people who were saved. After I observed these phenomena I went back to study the Bible and church history. In the end I clearly saw that the problem was that the old way of meeting did not work and was not able to make people stay.

Our traditional way of meeting was to shut people's mouths so that the longer people met with us, the more they did not open their mouths. There is a Chinese saying that says, "A newborn calf does not fear the tiger." When the newly saved ones first came to the meetings, they were like little children, saying a few words. But sadly, after three to five years of meeting with us they would no longer say anything. The older they got, the more they did not speak. Under this kind of condition it was hard to bring in new ones, and it was even harder to make them stay. Hence, in the past when we preached the gospel, we may have baptized a hundred people, but less than ten stayed. For this reason we felt that we must change the system. Acts shows us that we should meet from house to house (2:46; 5:42; 20:20), so in light of this we will now change the system.

THE IMPACT OF THE NEW SYSTEM
AND OUR COMMISSION

Recently, there have been meetings in the communities. If the elderly saints have the burden, I hope they also would join these meetings to help those in the communities and to establish home meetings with them. This will be effective. During our history of more than thirty years in Taiwan, never before have we had twenty-four thousand people baptized in less than four months. We estimated that one out of every four baptized would remain, but the results have been beyond our estimation. Out of twenty-four thousand people who have been baptized, eight thousand have remained. This does not, however, mean that we lost sixteen thousand. Some of the ones baptized have been unable to come into our midst for a time because of certain situations such as moving. Through our one-on-one visitations, five thousand out of these eight thousand people have already signed up. The first cause of this impact was our door-knocking, and the second cause was the continuous labor of the trainees who sacrificed their Lord's Day meetings to meet with the new ones in their homes. This is inspiring and encouraging.

PRAYERS FOR THE NEW SYSTEM AND FOR THE LABOR

We have seen that the change in system is necessary. Through much fellowship we have more or less entered into this burden. I hope that the older saints would take the lead to pray for those who have received the burden to visit and take care of the new ones and for the commission that these ones have received. I also hope that you would try your best to join the group meetings and to pay attention to the group meetings. We have to realize that our gatherings in the homes are more important than the big meetings at the meeting halls. We have said earlier that big meetings and small meetings go together like the two wings of a 747 airplane. If an airplane had only one wing, the airplane would not be able to take off. Two wings are required for an airplane to fly. The small meetings are the base, and the big meetings are the harvest.

The basis of a big meeting hall is the homes, just as the basic unit of a nation is the home. Without homes, a society has no basis. Without homes, a nation also has no basis. Hence, we must first establish the homes. Only in the homes can we produce people, and only in the homes can we beget, nourish, and teach people. I hope that the begetting, nourishing, and teaching would all be done in the homes. Thus, the elders of all the halls must lead and oversee the saints so that they would have at least one small group meeting a week. You may be exempt from other things but not from the small group meetings.

PAYING ATTENTION TO THE SMALL GROUP MEETINGS AND SPEAKING THE LORD'S WORD IN THE MEETINGS

We have a kind of slogan that says, "Heaven may fade, and earth may flee, but small group meetings must never be missed." However, based on my observation, the taste of our small group meetings is not strong enough. In the big meetings there are people who release messages to us, and once a message is given, the taste is strong. But when we gather in the homes, we are accustomed to not speaking. Thus, you do not speak, I do not speak, nor do the other brothers speak. In the end we can only look at each other, eat some dessert, and drink some water. There is not much taste to our meetings. There is a co-worker serving in the United States in the city of San Francisco whose father is in a denomination where they have also adopted the way of small group meetings. This co-worker's father was assigned to lead a small group, and he told his son that when they came together, none of them spoke. Eventually, everyone left and felt that they did not need this kind of meeting because no one spoke.

For a small group meeting to be enjoyable and rich, we must have the Lord's word. There are some saints among us who never speak, but if they were to open their mouths, the meeting would be enriched. The truths among us are pure, all-inclusive, and rich. We have the truths concerning the cross, resurrection, the Spirit, life, the church, the essence of the church, the testimony of the church, and the ground of the church. We may say that we are a literate family. Now we have to grasp the opportunity to exercise to speak the word of God. We have the riches, and we also have the utterance. I believe that as long as we all exercise properly, we will all be able to speak for the Lord.

Now I would like to have some fellowship with you and to make a request of you. First, I hope that all of us would change our concept to pay more attention to the small groups than to the big meetings. This does not mean that we should not have big meetings but that we should put more emphasis on the small group meetings than on the big meetings. Second, from now on all the elderly saints must renew their youth and learn to speak for the Lord. They all have the word in them and are rich inwardly. Now they simply need to learn to speak. I hope that all the elderly saints would go to the small group meetings to speak for the Lord.

Pray-reading was brought in among us in Tainan in 1965. The year after, in 1966, we began to call on the Lord in Los Angeles. Later, in 1968 we developed the practice of speaking in the meetings. This encouraged everyone. I remember one time in a meeting on the Lord's Day morning in Los Angeles when I asked everyone, "Do you know what to say after you are saved?" Then I continued, "At least you know how to say four words. The first word is *O,* the second word is *Lord,* the third word is *Amen,* and the fourth word is *Hallelujah.* O Lord, Amen, Hallelujah." From that day on, the words *O Lord, Amen, Hallelujah* became a short hymn. Whenever we sang that hymn, the meeting was enlivened.

When you come to the meeting, you may try to stand up to speak a few phrases such as, "O Lord, thank You that You are so good!" Then you may try to say something a little deeper such as, "O Lord, thank You that You are so good. You are my life." If you had an experience, you may speak your experience. For example, perhaps you were not happy in the morning and felt that things were not going smoothly. Usually in such a case you would grumble. But that morning when you were about to grumble, you began to call inwardly, saying, "O Lord." Then your grumbling disappeared, and your temper was gone because the Lord came in. This is a good and short experience. If ten people were meeting together, and everyone spoke briefly like this, the meeting would surely be fresh and living. This is the secret to a rich meeting.

A FEW PRACTICES CONCERNING
SPEAKING FOR THE LORD

We all can do this because none of us are newly saved. Even if we were newly saved, we still would have the essential characteristic in us of being able to speak for the Lord. However, when we speak, we should not tell long stories. Some saints either do not speak or once they begin speaking do not stop. They start with the first three generations of their ancestors and continue until everyone is bored. So remember that when speaking for the Lord, do not talk about your history. Instead, simply give a brief testimony. For example, you may say, "This morning I was not that happy, but once I thought about the Lord Jesus and called on Him, my inner being was soothed, and I began to sing. Thus, this whole day I have been very joyful." This is a good speaking.

Moreover, it is also good to speak about our experience of salvation. For example, you may say, "Thank the Lord! I had been worshipping idols for forty-eight years. One day the brothers and sisters from the church came to knock on my door and spoke to me from *The Mystery of Human Life* for five minutes. Then I was enlightened. I felt that the Lord Jesus was very good, so I was baptized. In the past after telling a lie I could still live peacefully, but now if I tell a lie I feel sorrowful inwardly." This is a very good testimony of salvation. You do not need to tell the story from your birth or describe many unrelated processes. When we give a testimony, we are often afraid that people may not understand what we are saying, so we try to say more. When we speak for the Lord, we often think that people may not understand, so we want to teach them. However, this is not needed. When we speak in the meetings, we should not speak long. We should not shut our mouths, but neither should we speak without end.

We have all heard the story about D. L. Moody. He was very powerful in the gospel. Some saints who met with him often prayed without end. One time Brother Moody was leading a meeting in which a sister was praying in this way. Finally, he felt that he had waited too long and said to everyone, "Saints, while our dear sister is still praying, let us sing." We encounter similar situations all the time. Such situations are hard to deal with. Hence, in the meetings we have to avoid being silent while at the same time avoid speaking too long, telling stories, or giving our history. All these practices should be avoided. We should only speak the Lord Jesus and our experience of Him.

Besides speaking for the Lord, we all have to be responsible to bring people to the small group meetings. We should not bring unbelievers. Rather, we should bring those who believe. Today in Taiwan it is convenient to make phone calls to invite people. We do not need to wait until tomorrow to make a phone call. Today after the meeting we can call a saint who was not present. We may share with him the content of our fellowship. We may tell him that the brothers and sisters care for him and that we hope he can come to our small group meeting in two days. Then two days later, we may call him again to remind him in the morning in case he forgot. Then in the evening we may give him a third call, asking if he needs a ride to go to the meeting. This kind of care is very much needed.

We have to realize that nothing we do will be in vain. This is the noblest and the most valuable thing we can do. Preaching the gospel is the most glorious matter in the universe. We are bringing blessing, love, grace, and God's salvation to people's homes. Although we are knocking at people's doors, troubling and bothering them, we are actually giving them grace and the best book among the human race—the Bible. What we are doing is the best.

CHAPTER TWO

THE YOUNG PEOPLE BEING STRONG
TO OVERCOME THE EVIL ONE

THE THREE GROUPS OF PEOPLE IN THE CHURCH

The elderly saints among us are full of vigor and vitality, the working saints among us are like brave lions, and the young ones among us are lively and full of strength. First John 2:12-19 addresses the fathers, the young men, and the young children, classifying the saints in the church into these three categories. Verse 14a says, "I have written to you, fathers, because you know Him who is from the beginning." The word *fathers* refers to the believers who are mature in life. They are the qualified ones, the ones who know Him who is from the beginning. God the Father is even more qualified than the fathers are. This is the first category. Verse 14b says, "I have written to you, young men, because you are strong and the word of God abides in you and you have overcome the evil one." In the Bible the Lord Jesus as an overcomer is called the Lion of the tribe of Judah (Rev. 5:5). Hence, the overcomers are also like lions that overcome the evil one. This is the second category. The third category consists of the young children, such as the high school and junior high school saints. First John 2:13b says, "I write to you, young children, because you know the Father." Young children only know to call on their fathers and mothers. Thus, the young children in the church only know the Father.

NOT LOVING THE WORLD

First John 2:12-14 shows that there are clear distinctions among the fathers, the young men, and the young children. Then verses 15 to 17 say, "Do not love the world nor the things in the world. If anyone loves the world, love for the Father is not in him; because all that is in the world, the lust of the flesh and the lust of the eyes and the vainglory of life, is not of the Father but is of the world. And the world is passing away, and its lust, but he who does the will of God abides forever." This passage explains what it means to overcome the evil one. The evil one is in the world. Hence, we should not love the world. What is the world? It is all that is in the world—the lust of the flesh, the lust of the eyes, and the vainglory of life. Vainglory is empty pride. The vainglory of life includes all the things that we boast of in the present life. All these things will pass away. If we are in all these things, we are not in the Father and do not love the Father. If we love the world, then God's love, the love for God, is not in us.

The last part of verse 17 says, "But he who does the will of God abides forever." To be for the Lord does not mean that we merely obey the will of God but that we do the will of God. If I charge you to do something, if you are to obey, you must do it. To do something is to carry out and accomplish a certain goal or purpose. The will of God is a goal or purpose, and when we carry it out, we are doing the will of God. Only those who do the will of God abide forever.

Verses 12 through 28 are divided into three sections in the Recovery Version. In these three sections, the fathers, the young men, and the young children are mentioned repeatedly. The first two times the apostle writes to these three groups of people, his speaking to the fathers is simple. Both times he speaks the same thing to them, saying that he writes to them and has written to them because they know Him who is from the beginning. As to the young men, his first speaking to them is simple, but his second speaking is not that simple. In his second speaking he says, "You are strong and the word of God abides in you and you have overcome the evil one"; he also tells them not to love the world (vv. 14b-15a). This reveals the goal of overcoming and the reason why many do not overcome. It also reveals that the obstacles that we must overcome in this warfare are in the world. In the world are the lust of the flesh, the lust of the eyes, and the boast, vainglory, and pride of the present life. These are the appropriate words that the Lord has given us today.

THE CHURCHES IN TAIWAN BEING RICH IN RESOURCES

Some people have asked us why we have different levels of meetings among us, such as the meeting for the elderly saints and the meeting for the working saints. We decided to change our system three years ago because now the goal is to gospelize Taiwan. In gospelizing Taiwan we do not want to merely preach the gospel all over Taiwan. Rather, we want to saturate Taiwan with the gospel. This will require the cooperation of all the saints. The reason we chose Taiwan to be the first place, the starting point, for our gospelization was that even though the Lord's recovery has already reached the six continents, only Taiwan has the deep capacity to be gospelized.

According to the statistics we gathered four years ago, there were around 610 local churches all over the globe. Now the number has increased to over 900. Among all these local churches, why did we choose to start the evangelization with the churches in Taiwan and not in another place such as the United States? The reason was that although Taiwan is not big and cannot be compared with the United States in size, Taiwan has the deepest capacity and the richest background. In other words, Taiwan truly has a rich heritage and abundant resources.

For instance, recently we held a large-scale gospel meeting in China Stadium for the high school and junior high school students. During our preparation we estimated that around six thousand people would come, but in the end over fifteen thousand came, which was one and a half times more than what we had expected. Hence, we have been inwardly enlightened that the Lord has chosen Taiwan, and we thank the Lord for bringing us to Taiwan and making Taiwan the birthplace of our gospelization work. Taiwan is rich in "minerals." Since Taiwan is so rich in resources, we have to "mine" and dig up these resources.

Let us consider another example. In the most recent meeting for the elderly saints we expected to have five or six hundred people and thought that most of them would come late. However, fifteen minutes before the meeting was to begin all the elderly saints had arrived. When we entered the meeting, they were already singing and were full of vigor, just like the young people in the young people's meetings. Their youth had been renewed. Hence, even the meetings for the elderly saints are a huge "gold mine" for us to dig. We should dig the "gold mine" of the elderly saints in every meeting hall. We do not mean that we should ask them for gold to build a big meeting hall but that we should cause each one of them to be living. It is the same with the young people's meetings. The number attending these meetings is quite high. They truly are the young people. They are like a neat and orderly army. The churches in Taiwan are rich in capital and should be developed.

MOTIVATING THE SAINTS
WHO ARE TEACHERS AND MEDICAL PERSONNEL
TO DO THE WORK OF GAINING PEOPLE

Whom should we motivate? We have to motivate all the teachers in the whole province. We have around three thousand teachers working in kindergartens, elementary schools, junior high schools, high schools, and colleges. This situation has much potential. If these three thousand teachers were all motivated, what kind of an effect would they produce in the schools? The fifteen thousand high school and junior high school students who came to the last gospel meeting were brought mostly by their teachers. Some teachers brought a hundred students while some brought fifty. On the other hand, we also have close to one hundred fifty medical personnel, including doctors, nurses, and technicians. They have not taken any action for quite a while and have reserved quite a bit of strength. If this strength were motivated, it would be a great thing. So we have to motivate the teachers to gain their students and the medical staff to gain their patients. This would be very worthwhile.

In the past two years of training we have had seven to eight hundred people each term, and they all had a goal and a method to go door-knocking. Yesterday I received a cable from Ghana, Africa. The saints there went out to knock on doors for three days. There were 140 saints who went out for four hours each day. In three days 1,300 were saved, and 545 were baptized. In our past two years of door-knocking in Taipei, we also have had many sweet stories. The saints spoke *The Mystery of Human Life* to the taxi drivers while commuting from Hall One to Hall Three, and some were saved and baptized. The number of taxi drivers who were baptized as a result of our preaching may have exceeded 500. There were brothers and sisters everywhere in Taipei. Many of them had stopped meeting for a long time, but through our door-knocking and contact they were brought back. Therefore, we surely must dig this gold mine of Taiwan.

THE YOUNG PEOPLE OVERCOMING THE EVIL ONE

The passage in 1 John 2 is very precious. It has several features. Concerning the fathers, it says that they know Him who is from the beginning. Concerning the young children, it says that they know the Father. These two groups are quite simple. But regarding the middle category of the young men, it says that they overcame the evil one. God has a goal on the earth, which is to defeat His enemy. Here the Bible does not mention the name "Satan"; instead, it mentions his nature and what he does, saying that he is the evil one. In Greek the phrase *evil one* is a particular, emphatic phrase denoting that he is absolutely evil and is contagious and influential. In Greek there are several words that mean "evil," but the word used here is the severest one. It implies that after this evil one infects others, he causes them to do evil things as well. After this evil infects others, it does not cause them to die immediately. Rather, it attacks people inwardly, causing them to become insane, to turn bad, and to be unable to live at peace. Thus, it is truly evil.

THE LOVE OF GOD BEING THE MOTIVATION

In the Lord's prayer the Lord says, "And do not bring us into temptation, but deliver us from the evil one" (Matt. 6:13a). Some translations render the phrase *the evil one* as *the evil,* but actually, the evil here refers to the evil one. The evil one is God's enemy, who is evil and fierce. God's goal is to have the young men deal with His enemy so that His purpose will be attained. The source of this motivation is God's love. First John 2:15 says regarding anyone who loves the world that "love for the Father is not in him." This is a good translation, but it is not a literal translation of the original expression. The literal translation of this verse is "the love of the Father is not in him." The phrase *love of the Father* implies that the Father's love is within us, causing us to love the Father, that is, to love God. The Father's love, or God's love, in man is the motivation, the source of love. The power with which the young men overcome Satan is God's love, which also causes them to love God. Actually, it is not we who love God but something in us called God's love. Satan is evil, whereas God is love. Evil infects people, causing them to not have peace and to do bad things that affect others and causes them to not have peace. On the contrary, God's love within us is a motivating power that gives us rest and peace.

Here we can see a contrast. On the one hand there is Satan, and on the other hand there is God's love, and both are active. In the New Testament we see that while evil is very active, love is also very active. Love is our motivation, giving us patience and endurance. Mothers love their children and even give up their lives because of love. A newspaper once reported a plane crash in which only a child survived because his mother had embraced him during the disaster in order to protect him. This is love. God loves us; He is love. God's love is in us and operates in us. The result of this operation is that we love God and man.

THE LOVE OF GOD CAUSING MAN
TO LOVE THE WORD OF GOD

Not only so, all those who love God also love the word of God. When God's love operates in us, we also love and desire God's word. We have God's love and God's word in us, and as a result, this makes us strong. What does it mean for us to be strong? To be strong means that even though there are many things and matters that oppose God, we are still able to stand. We are like a seed that has been planted into the ground and that passes through the immense pressure of layers of soil and grows up from the ground. This is similar to how a small seedling is able to break open the earth's crust and grow up. The life strength in a small seedling is very strong.

THE REAL SITUATION OF THE WORLD

The young men were the second category of people that John lists. They have God's love and God's word within them. They are strong and nothing can overcome them. The greater the pressure and the opposition, the more powerful they become. They do not love the world because they have love within. This love causes them not to love the world or to turn to the world but to turn to God. The world is against God. Wherever the world is, God is not, and wherever God is, the world is not. John uses a brief description to describe all these conditions in a thorough way. In speaking of the world and the things in the world, he mentions the lust of the flesh, the lust of the eyes, and the vainglory, pride, and boast of the present life.

The lives of people in Taiwan today include many things that far exceed the basic necessities of living. The things that exceed the basic necessities of living may be described as the lust of the flesh, the lust of the eyes, and the vainglory of life. When rich people invite others for a meal, they must take them to a high-class restaurant. If the price of the meal is too low in a certain restaurant, they will not take them then. Fifty years ago in Shanghai, the biggest metropolis in China, a wealthy person would pay five hundred dollars for a piece of clothing. A few days later, another wealthy person would wear an almost identical piece of clothing, but would pay double the price for it. These kinds of people wear clothing not to keep warm but for the pride and vainglory of life. Whether we are speaking of Shanghai in the past or Taipei in the present, many department stores have made money from the pride of life. Rich people also like to have expensive French or German cars. It is not that these cars are not good but that they show man's pride of life.

THE WORLD BEING IN OPPOSITION TO GOD'S WILL

To meet the needs of our living, we all have to work. But we do not need to work more than eight hours a day to meet the needs of our living. To work eight hours a day is sufficient to properly meet the needs of our living, but to work over eight hours is to waste our effort and to sell ourselves. Some nurses in the United States work overtime every day. They are selling their lives and themselves. In Revelation 18 Babylon the Great sells all kinds of items, such as ivory and precious stone, but the last item is the souls of men (vv. 12-13). In Taiwan a husband and a wife can make a living as a couple by working five to six days a week. If this is enough to make a living, why do many still work overtime? Of course, everyone has his own reasons—a need in the company or a special need in the family. However, I hope that we all would be clear that today we belong to the Lord. On the one hand we need to work, but on the other hand we should work only to meet the needs of our living. What remains should be for the Lord's use. We are not for the world's use. Even if the world were to offer us a lot of money, we would not sell ourselves.

If we work eight hours a day, five and a half days a week, we should be able to earn more than enough for our living. If we, because of working overtime, do not read our Bible, go to the meetings, preach the gospel, and have the church life, then we are selling our souls. We are selling ourselves. We should see that in principle the career or business we have is our side job. If we take our business as our main job, then our business becomes something of the world, that is, the lust of the flesh, the lust of the eyes, and the vainglory of life. The will of the Father is completely contradictory to these things. We must be clear that these two lusts plus the vainglory in the world oppose the will of God all the time.

THE WILL OF GOD BEING TO OBTAIN A BODY

What is the will of God? Some people wonder whether it is the will of God for them to get married earlier or later, and others wonder if it is the will of God for them to marry this brother or that sister. These are all trivial matters and actually have little to do with the will of God. The will of God, according to the New Testament, is firstly for us to be saved. God does not want us to obey the Ten Commandments or to do anything else. Rather, He only wants us to take one way, which is to believe in Jesus that we would be saved and receive the eternal life. Secondly, the will of God is for us to love the Lord and to love God. At the end of the Gospels, the Lord asked Peter, "Do you love Me more than these?" (John 21:15). When we believe in the Lord and love the Lord, we will follow the Lord.

What should we do to follow the Lord? When I was saved, I read a word about following the Lord, but I did not know how to follow Him. Romans 12 says, "And do not be fashioned according to this age, but be transformed by the renewing of the mind that you may prove what the will of God is, that which is good and well pleasing and perfect" (v. 2). Strictly speaking, the will of God is that we who are saved, who love Him, and who follow Him, would live a normal church life. When we are properly living in the Body of Christ, we are following the Lord, obeying the will of God, and doing the will of God. Today God is doing one thing on the earth—He is building up the church and perfecting the Body of Christ. He has to gain a Body. This is the will of God.

BEING BRANCHES THAT BEAR FRUIT

Today if what we are doing is not related to this, we are not doing the will of God. We should live in the church and practice the Body life. This is to do the will of God. The first thing we should do in the church life is bring people to salvation. Preaching the gospel to bring people to salvation is our obligatory commission. We are the branches of the Lord as the vine, and since we are branches, we have to bear fruit. The branches of the vine are not for producing blossoms for people's appreciation but for bearing fruit. Our fruit is the saved ones, and our fruit-bearing brings people to salvation. The tree of life bears new fruit every month, twelve times a year (Rev. 22:2). The vine should bear clusters of fruit.

Today in every place the rate at which the number of saved ones is increasing is very slow. The Lord's recovery in the English-speaking world has been spreading from the United States for more than twenty years and has added more than six hundred churches with an average of around 100 to 150 saints in each locality. However, this rate of increase is not very fast. The result of our study has found that we have not been bearing fruit properly because our way of meeting is wrong and the form of our church life has become rigid. In most of our church meetings, one person speaks and everyone else listens. This nullifies the function of the saints, causing them to be unable to bear remaining fruit. I hope that from now on when we come to the small group meetings, we all would speak for five minutes at the most. We do not need to speak too much. In this way our meetings will be full of liveliness and vitality.

VISITING PEOPLE AND SAVING PEOPLE BY DOOR-KNOCKING

Today the gospel preaching in Christianity lacks power. Not many people are saved through it, and of those who are saved, not many remain. It is the same among us. The main reason is that the way we meet is wrong. The Lord is showing us the way of door-knocking. This is not a common kind of door-knocking, so we all must be trained. We have had two terms of training during which 800 trainees visited 24,000 people. We not only knocked on doors, but we also had home meetings to keep the saved ones.

In the past we spent enormous amounts of effort to bring people to the church and to baptize them, but after less than two weeks, they were gone. There have been around 100,000 people who were baptized in Taipei, but now less than 5,000 are meeting. There have been seventy to eighty thousand people who were baptized in other areas of the island, but now only three to four thousand are meeting. Where are the rest of them? We often meet many people in various professions who are our brothers and sisters, but they are not meeting. What is the reason for this? The reason is that the way we meet is not proper and makes it hard for people to stay. This may be likened to spending much effort to give birth to a child but abandoning him afterward. This is a pitiful situation.

Whether or not the gospelization of Taiwan can be successful hinges on the young people. The young people are the pillars of the church. They have to take up the responsibility to do God's will. God's will is for us to live the church life; this is our main job. Today we must clearly see that the best way to preach the gospel and deliver the gospel is to visit people by door-knocking. This is the pattern that the Lord left us. The Lord Himself came to the earth from heaven and visited us personally. Since He visited us, we also need to visit people and preach the gospel to them. After we have baptized people, we should meet with them at home. We do not need to fear that we will not have anything to say. We simply have to go, and the Lord will give us the word to speak.

HAVING HOME MEETINGS IN PEOPLE'S HOMES

Once a person is saved through our door-knocking, we need to meet with him in his home the next day. If we meet with him in this way, we will be able to gain his household. Two households may then be combined together to be a small group. Then several small groups may be gathered together in a way similar to our meetings in the meeting hall. In this way we will surely be very busy, because we will be doing God's will all day long. In addition, we will spontaneously have no time, interest, or taste to take care of the things of the world. "The world is passing away, and its lust, but he who does the will of God abides forever" (1 John 2:17). I believe that we are all wise and that we want to seek the things that will last forever. What lasts forever? Only the will of God lasts forever. This is our commission, our will, and our main job.

Never fear that you will lose your job or that you will lack something in your living if you do this. In my journey of following the Lord for sixty years, I have never seen a person who, because of his love for the Lord, was unable to make a living. If we would say, "O Lord, I do not want anything else; I just love You," then the Lord would say, "I will give you whatever you ask of Me." This is real. Some people have asked me, "Mr. Lee, you believe in Jesus, but does He take care of your meals?" I dare not answer whether Jesus takes care of my meals or not. But I can testify that if you truly love Jesus, He will not only take care of your meals, but He will also take care of the meals of your offspring for thousands of generations. Jehovah promised this to His people, saying, "Showing lovingkindness to thousands of generations of those who love Me" (Exo. 20:6; Deut. 5:10). Our God is omnipotent; nothing is impossible with Him.

PREACHING THE GOSPEL
AT WORK AND IN OUR LIVING

The prosperity of Taiwan today is due to the presence of the church. The more we love the Lord, the more Taiwan will be blessed. Many years ago when I was in England, I applied for visas to Denmark, the Netherlands, and Belgium. The Belgian who worked in the embassy asked where I came from, and when I told him that I came from Taiwan, he did not even know where Taiwan was. The whole world can testify that they never expected Taiwan to develop to such a degree, especially in its economic achievements. The main reason for this development is that there are people here who love the Lord. This is the main factor for Taiwan's being blessed. Hence, do not worry. You should have a job to support your family, but you also have to live the church life. If you are working, you have to preach the gospel to your colleagues in addition to working with them. For example, you can preach the gospel during your break in the afternoon. Preaching the gospel should be our occupation, our main job. Our preaching of the gospel sows the seeds. One day the seeds may sprout and grow.

We need our view to be broadened to see that the church life is not merely meetings in the meeting hall. We long to see the day when there will be two hundred thousand homes in Taipei with home meetings. At that time, when we go to a store to buy something, we will meet the brothers and sisters. When we go to school, we will also meet the brothers and sisters. When we go to Tainan or Taipei, we will also meet the brothers and sisters. In this way Christians will be all over the earth, and our brothers and sisters will be everywhere. This responsibility lies upon us, and especially upon the young people. We all have to see that taking this new way will bring us back to the proper church life that we may do God's will.

God's will is for us to preach the gospel every day and to bring people to salvation. We should not go door-knocking merely for a week or two. Rather, we need to go out every day to knock on doors and to preach the gospel. Once people are saved, we should have home meetings with them. When we meet with them, we will spontaneously learn many things, such as how to lead them, how to supply them, how to open the way for them, how to open their understanding, how to help them to know the Holy Spirit, and how to teach them to pray. If we merely know these things but do not do them, there will be no effect. Only when we practice doing them will there be the result. If the young people rise up, the new way would surely be successful.

CHAPTER THREE

PRAYER AND FELLOWSHIP
REGARDING SPECIFIC WORKS

Scripture Reading: Matt. 6:31-33; Rom. 12:1-2, 11

SEEKING FIRST GOD'S KINGDOM
AND GOD'S RIGHTEOUSNESS

Matthew 6:31-32 says, "Therefore do not be anxious, saying, What shall we eat? or, What shall we drink? or, With what shall we be clothed? For all these things the Gentiles are anxiously seeking. For your heavenly Father knows that you need all these things." If we become anxious regarding what to eat and drink and what to wear, our eating, drinking and clothing will become our burden, and we will become the same as the Gentiles. Almost all human beings, regardless of place or time, are anxious for their living. Man's living cannot be separated from the two aspects of eating and clothing. Our eating signifies what we need inwardly, and our clothing signifies what we need outwardly.

Whether a person is rich or poor, he is anxious for his eating and clothing. No matter what a person's degree of eating and clothing is, this is an unalterable principle. However, the Lord Jesus said, "I say to you, Do not be anxious for your life, what you should eat or what you should drink; nor for your body, what you should put on" (v. 25). This is the Lord's command, the Lord's charge. In verse 32a the Lord said, "For all these things the Gentiles are anxiously seeking." We do not need to imitate them. The second half of the verse says, "For your heavenly Father knows that you need all these things." This can be considered a fact or a promise.

As the head of the household, every proper father cares for

his whole family, including his children. In the spiritual realm we also have a Father, the heavenly Father, who knows all of our needs. However, we may have never treasured this word in Matthew 6. We need to thank the Father for this, saying, "O Father, I really worship You. Thank You, Father. If I become anxious concerning what to eat and what to put on, I will offend You because this is what the Gentiles do. They do not have a heavenly Father, so they are anxious for themselves. But this should not be the case with me. I have a heavenly Father. I do not need to be anxious for all these things because You know everything." In verses 31-32a the Lord gives us a command, saying, "Do not be anxious, saying, What shall we eat? or, What shall we drink? or, With what shall we be clothed? For all these things the Gentiles are anxiously seeking." We should not follow the custom of the Gentiles, being anxious about what to eat and drink and what to wear every day. This is what they talk about all the time. We have a heavenly Father, and He knows all that we need regarding food and clothing.

The Lord said, "But seek first His kingdom and His righteousness, and all these things will be added to you" (v. 33). Here it does not say that we need to beseech but to seek, meaning to find. What we seek should be God's kingdom and His righteousness. We not only need to pray or beseech, but we also need to find. We have to first find God's kingdom and His righteousness, and then what we need will be added to us. The first half of this word—"seek first His kingdom and His righteousness"—is a command, and the second half—"all these things will be added to you"—is a promise. He did not say that all these things would be given to us; He said that they would be added to us. Besides God's kingdom and God's righteousness, He has to add to us all these things. In a similar way, when we buy something at a store, the store may give us a small gift that does not cost anything. This is something added.

Today God's kingdom is the church, and God's righteousness is Christ. If we seek God's kingdom but are detached from the church and do not live the church life, then we are not truly seeking God's kingdom. Today God's kingdom is the church. Romans 14:17 says, "For the kingdom of God is not eating and drinking, but righteousness and peace and joy in the Holy Spirit." The kingdom of God is the church, and the righteousness of God is Christ. When we come to the church and live the church life, we are seeking the kingdom of God. When we live Christ, we are seeking God's righteousness. As a result, we have both the kingdom and righteousness. In other words, when we have the church life, we have Christ as well.

Does the heavenly Father give us only these things? No, He adds to us our food, our clothing, our transportation, our traveling, and our housing. All that we need regarding food, clothing, housing, and transportation are added to us. I have been saved for sixty-two years and have been serving the Lord for fifty-five years. I have never seen anyone who seeks God's kingdom and His righteousness suffer from hunger, coldness, or a lack of food, clothing, housing, or transportation. On the contrary, all those whom I saw were in the church, living Christ and living the kingdom life. Ultimately, they had God's kingdom and His righteousness, and God also added to them the four essential requirements for living—food, clothing, housing, and transportation. Hence, these three verses in Matthew 6 contain a command, a warning, a fact, and a promise.

PRESENTING OUR BODIES A LIVING SACRIFICE

Romans 12:1-2 says, "I exhort you therefore, brothers, through the compassions of God to present your bodies a living sacrifice, holy, well pleasing to God, which is your reasonable service. And do not be fashioned according to this age, but be transformed by the renewing of the mind that you may prove what the will of God is, that which is good and well pleasing and perfect." These verses first mention our bodies (v. 1) and then our mind in the soul (v. 2). Verse 11 goes on to speak about our spirit within. First we have to present our body. Then when we come to the church, our mind needs to be transformed through renewing. Our thinking needs to be changed, and our old mind needs to be renewed. Then we need to be burning in spirit, serving the Lord.

Today people all over the world are very busy. In a sense,

no one is free. Even beggars and idle people are very busy. However, we who love the Lord, in the midst of our busy lives, must present our bodies to the Lord and place ourselves in the church life. It is not enough to merely say that we have consecrated ourselves. We must practically present our bodies. We may spend about an hour traveling to and from the meeting each way and an hour in the meeting. These three hours we spend for the meeting are consecrated to the Lord. We need to pray to consecrate every meeting to the Lord.

Secular people are busy in the worldly things, but Christians should be busy in prayer. No matter how busy people are, they still have time to talk. They can spend a whole day talking on the phone. Once they start talking, they can talk for half an hour or an hour. If we would use the time that we spend on the phone to pray, we would have much time. To pray is to present our bodies. This is a battle. To make a phone call does not require any effort, but to pray requires much strength. We do not feel tired when we make a phone call, but once we begin to pray, we feel tired. Satan has many ways to keep us from praying. When we are not praying, no one comes to visit us. But once we kneel down to pray for five minutes, someone comes knocking on our door. Sometimes it may even be someone knocking on the wrong door. Once we are interrupted, we are unable to pray anymore, and it takes much effort to turn back to the spirit.

The fact that prayer is a battle shows us that presenting our bodies is also truly a battle. For us to waste things such as our money, time, and energy is very easy and does not require any effort. But when we want to accomplish something serious, we need to spend much effort and work hard. Children need to work hard and to set aside a time to study from 7 to 10 P.M., presenting their bodies to study for three hours. But if they gossip and talk, they will not work hard. We need to fight in order to present our bodies to meet and pray.

BEING TRANSFORMED
THROUGH THE RENEWING OF THE MIND

On the one hand, we need to present our bodies for the church life. On the other hand, there are still many old thoughts in our mind. We may be from the east, the west, the north, or the south, and we may have our own distinctions, customs, and regulations. However, the Lord has gathered us together in Christ, so we should not have any distinctions. Hence, our mind needs to be transformed by the renewing. In 1962 when I first went to America to begin the work there, the first two years I traveled all over the United States. The people there often said that I did not seem like a Chinese person because I ate what they ate and drank what they drank. Even though I did not like coffee, because they drank coffee, I also drank a little. We all love the Lord and are living in the church life, but we all have different dispositions. Eventually, our opinions and concepts may come out, causing many differences and problems among us. Therefore, we need our concepts to be changed. We need to be transformed by the renewing of the mind.

BEING BURNING IN SPIRIT, SERVING THE LORD

Very often we present our bodies and have some renewing and transformation in our mind, but our spirit is very cold, not burning. We do not pray, read the Bible, preach the gospel, or take care of people. It seems as if we do not want to do anything. This is abnormal. A normal Christian should possess three things: a presented body, a renewed and transformed mind, and a burning spirit. If we are not burning in our spirit, we will not pray or open our mouths when we come to the meeting. In the end, we will let the "shepherds" among us pray and speak for everyone. However, if we all are burning in spirit, then when you pray, I will also pray. Everyone will function, not wanting to be left behind, and the meeting will be sweet and rich. Thus, we all need to present our bodies, be renewed and transformed in our mind, and be burning in our spirit.

The most difficult matter in us is our mind. When there is a problem in the church, it usually comes from our mind. If we did not love the Lord and came to the meetings only once a year, there would be no problems in the church. But when we are raised up to love the Lord, to present our bodies, and to meet daily, we have more and more opinions. One day we may say that the chair arrangement is not right, and the next day we may say that the curtains were not hung properly. It may seem to us that there are many things that are wrong. Before we did not come to clean, but once we come we begin to have many ideas. We may think that the rags are not right because we should not use damp rags or that the brooms are not right because we should not use hard brooms. We were peaceful when we were not knocking on doors, but once we go out to knock on doors, we have no peace. We may say that our partners walk too fast or that they ring the doorbell for too long. All of our opinions come out. When we did not love the Lord, there were no problems because we stayed at home. However, once we begin to love the Lord, it seems that everyone is wrong and only we ourselves are right. Our mind is very hard to deal with. We need the Lord to be merciful to us, to grant us sufficient grace, to renew and transform us, and to make us burning in spirit.

BEING BURDENED TO PRAY
FOR SPECIFIC AREAS OF THE WORK

Some elderly saints have asked what they should do in the new way. In short, all the elderly saints should spend at least fifteen minutes a day to pray. They need to have a set time—perhaps at four o'clock in the morning, three o'clock in the afternoon, or eight o'clock in the evening—to present their bodies to pray with a burning spirit, without their own opinions, and absolutely according to God's will. In their prayer they do not need to pray for their family members one by one. Rather, they should stand on the promise of Matthew 6, praying, "O Lord, I pray for Your kingdom and Your righteousness concerning all of the needs in our family. You are my Father. You know all things, and You must add to me what we need. Please remember me." This is enough. Neither do the elderly saints need to pray for their son's studies. Rather, they only need to say, "O Lord, You know what my son needs and what kind of circumstances he encounters. Please add what is needed to me." We only need to pray for His kingdom and the church. In every single Epistle that Paul wrote he asked the receivers to pray regarding the word of God and spiritual matters. In none of his Epistles did he tell people to pray for their family affairs.

The elderly saints need first to set aside a fixed time, rain or shine, to pray for the church and to have much fellowship. For example, while the trainees go door-knocking in the communities, bringing people to salvation and baptizing some, the elderly saints should receive the fellowship to pray for these matters. Second, they need to pray for all the home meetings. Third, they should pray for the discussion meetings for the freshmen in college, through which we hope to baptize over a thousand people before school starts. Fourth, the gospel work in the high schools is very active, and many of the teachers have been raised up to be burdened for the gospel. All of this requires the prayer of the churches.

Moreover, there are also many saints who are doctors and nurses. In the Military General Hospital alone there are one hundred fifty saints. If all these doctors and nurses were burning in spirit, the gospelization of Taiwan would be accomplished very soon. Hence, for the gospelization of Taiwan, we need to do several things simultaneously. We also should not forget to promote the children's meeting as one of the items for our prayer. All those who have an understanding of spiritual matters know that the prayers of the believers before the Lord are very crucial and valuable. Without our prayer, God is unable to do anything. A certain saint once said that our prayer is like the tracks for God's train. Wherever the tracks have been laid, there the train can go. God's will is like a train, and our prayers are like the tracks. If we do not lay the tracks for God's will, the train of God's will is unable to move. Thus, there are at least seven major items for which the elderly saints should spend time to pray every day—the door-knocking in the communities, the home meetings in the communities, the gospel work at the colleges, the gospel work at the junior high and high schools, the rising up of the teachers in the junior high and high schools, the rising up of the medical personnel, and the children's work. We need to love the Lord, live for the Lord, and live to the Lord. If we receive this burden to spend at least ten to fifteen minutes each day to pray, the church in Taipei will be changed in half a year. The more tracks we lay, and the farther and broader we lay them, the more God's will can move on the earth without obstruction.

SPEAKING IN THE SMALL GROUP MEETINGS

The one thing we must pay particular attention to when we go to a small group meeting is that we all have to speak. If we do not speak, we kill the meeting and nullify our function. We need to function by speaking. The more we speak, the more we will know how to speak. On the contrary, the less we speak, the less we will know how to speak. However, when we speak, we should not speak nonsense. We have to speak using simple and concise words. When the day of our group meeting comes, we have to pray to the Lord throughout the day, "O Lord, today I have to speak for You in the small group meeting. Please give me a word." We may find an appropriate word from the verses that we pray-read each day, and we may speak for two minutes at the most. If there are ten or twenty people meeting and each speaks for two minutes, then each one will have three chances to speak. This kind of meeting will be a new, living, and profitable meeting.

The spirit of the new way is to allow each saint to have the opportunity to function and to open his or her mouth to speak for the Lord. We all have to be encouraged to change our old habit of not speaking and prepare before the meeting to speak in the meeting. In our preparation we may find the main points or the paragraphs with which we were touched and for which we have a feeling. Never speak nonsense. Rather, we have to speak from the Word of God. The more we speak, the more inspiration we will have, and the more we will supply others. I hope that we all would practice this matter.

A CHRISTIAN GROUP IN BRAZIL

In 1965 I went to Sao Paulo, Brazil. The Catholic Church there was very cold, and the Protestant churches and denominations were very dead. Only one group, called "The Christian Assembly," was burning. They had three hundred thousand saints, thirty thousand of whom were in Sao Paulo alone.

They did not have people giving sermons in their meetings. In their meetings on Lord's Day morning someone would call a hymn, and they would all sing together. The more they sang, the stronger their spirits would become. After they sang, they would pray for almost half an hour. Everyone prayed; no one led the meeting. After they prayed, they would testify and share. There were two microphones in the meeting place—the brothers lined up behind one, and the sisters lined up behind the other. They sat separately in the meeting; there was a clear distinction in their seating arrangement. The sisters wore proper clothing and did not wear any makeup. The brothers and sisters gave their testimonies during the entire time, and after their testimonies, they asked for those who wanted to be baptized. There was a large baptistery on the platform, and whoever had brought a new one was responsible to baptize him. They did not require any particular fellowship before the baptisms. Sometimes they would baptize around ten people, and at other times they would baptize over one hundred. They had baptisms every Lord's Day. After the baptisms, a responsible one would take the lead to read two or three verses, point out the main point of the verses, and end the meeting.

They did not have many big gospel meetings, Bible-study meetings, or prayer meetings. They had a big meeting only on the Lord's Day. During the week they would meet in the homes, from house to house. In this way they met and brought people to be saved. When there were too many people in a home, they would open another one. Gradually, they baptized many people. This way of preaching the gospel and bringing people to salvation is very effective and makes it easy for people to stay because this kind of gospel preaching brings people in one by one. Eventually many people are brought in and stay.

EVERYONE PAYING ATTENTION
TO THE HOME MEETINGS

We must acknowledge that the big meetings we had in the past where one person spoke and everyone else listened made it difficult to bring people to be saved and to cause them to stay. This does not mean that we should not have big, corporate meetings but that it is more important to have home meetings every week. This will cause all of us to be burning together and to bring people to salvation. Furthermore, we must see that door-knocking is a very effective way to preach the gospel. If we do this, it will not be uncommon to have a twofold or fourfold increase in number. I hope the elderly saints would take the lead to be changed in their concepts, be renewed and transformed in their mind, and not focus on the big meetings all the time. For the benefit of God's house and God's kingdom, we must change our ways. The elderly saints should take the lead to have a set time of prayer every day and should attend the small group meetings every week. In the small group meetings everyone should speak but not give long speeches. Everyone should function, help others to function, and perfect one another.

SPECIFIC AREAS OF THE WORK

Regarding door-knocking, every one of us should go to knock on doors at least once a week. Do not go this week because you are happy and then refuse to go the next week because you are not happy. We have to do this in a consistent way. We have to go door-knocking every week for two hours each time. We should first knock on the doors in the surrounding area, such as the doors of our neighbors and relatives. Then we should go to the people on the streets and in the communities. Week by week we must knock on doors near and far. If we all do this together, we would be able to bring in many saved ones. Once someone is saved, we need to start a home meeting. Then we need to go door-knocking again, and then we will begin another home meeting. This should be our normal service.

In the past the children's meeting was always held in the meeting hall and was mostly led by the young people. Now the gospel work on the college campuses and at the junior high and high schools is very active, and the young people all have specific services in this work. Thus, they cannot take care of the children anymore. Hence, we need to rely on the elderly saints to spend the time and effort to teach the children. We may divide the children into two or three levels. Some saints will need to work on the lesson materials, and some need to tell the stories. Children ages 4 through 6 may be on the first level. With these ones you only need to sing hymns with them and tell them stories. Children ages 7 through 9 may be on the second level. With these ones you need to teach them something, which may require some lesson materials. Children ages 10 through 12 may be on the third level. With them you need lesson materials to help teach them something deeper. The elderly saints may use their homes. After the children get off from school, the elderly saints may open their homes and prepare some snacks to welcome them. Then they may sing with the children, tell them stories, and lead them to know God.

Every one of us should be able to do these three things—pray every day, join the small group meetings, and go door-knocking and have home meetings every week. The fourth matter is taking care of the children. I hope that more people will receive the burden to open their homes to take care of the children. Twenty years ago I said that we should have ten thousand children in Taipei, and then ten years later we would have ten thousand young brothers and sisters. If the saints had taken this word and practiced it, we would have twenty to thirty thousand young people today. Moreover, gaining people in this way is very safe, because they are taught by us and receive the gospel from us from their youth. Thus, they should be very solid. If this were the case, many young saints would not need to put aside their gospel work at school to do the children's work. I hope that from now on the elderly saints would pick up the burden and take the lead to do this in their homes. The effect will be very promising in the long run.

CHAPTER FOUR

SEEKING GOD'S KINGDOM
AND GOD'S RIGHTEOUSNESS

Scripture Reading: Luke 14:26-35; 2 Pet. 1:3-4; Matt. 6:31-33

GOD HAVING GRANTED TO US ALL THINGS
WHICH RELATE TO LIFE AND GODLINESS

Luke 14:26-35 says, "If anyone comes to Me and does not hate his own father and mother and wife and children and brothers and sisters, and moreover, even his own soul-life, he cannot be My disciple. Whoever does not carry his own cross and come after Me cannot be My disciple. For which of you, wanting to build a tower, does not first sit down and calculate the cost, whether he has enough to complete it? Lest perhaps, once he has laid a foundation and is not able to finish, all those looking on will begin to mock him, saying, This man began to build and was not able to finish. Or what king, going to engage another king in war, will not first sit down and deliberate whether he is able with ten thousand to meet the one coming against him with twenty thousand? Otherwise, while he is yet at a distance, he sends an envoy and asks for the terms of peace. In the same way therefore everyone of you who does not forsake all his own possessions cannot be My disciple. Therefore salt is good; but if even the salt becomes tasteless, with what will its saltiness be restored? It is fit neither for the land nor for the manure pile; they will throw it out. He who has ears to hear, let him hear." When people hear this passage, they often find it difficult to take, because what is spoken of in this portion is very high and absolute.

It is normal for a pursuing Christian to believe and obey the Lord's word before Him and to live and act according to

His word. However, the requirements in Luke 14 seem too high. Verse 26 says that if we do not hate our own father, mother, wife, children, brothers, sisters, and even our own soul-life, we cannot be the Lord's disciples. Who can do this? Even if we already hated people, we would not be able to hate to the degree that we would hate our own relatives, including our parents, our children, our wife, and our brothers and sisters. The Lord used the examples of building a tower and engaging in war to ask those who were following Him to calculate the cost (vv. 28-32). It seems that there is no way for us to follow the Lord, because if we want to follow Him, we have to hate all the people, things, and matters that are related to us.

However, 2 Peter 1:3-4 says, "Seeing that His divine power has granted to us all things which relate to life and godliness, through the full knowledge of Him who has called us by His own glory and virtue, through which He has granted to us precious and exceedingly great promises that through these you might become partakers of the divine nature, having escaped the corruption which is in the world by lust." The precious divine power has granted to us all things which relate to life and godliness. Therefore, it is not we ourselves who do anything or leave anything. Rather, the life in us does everything. We may be unable to get through in Luke 14, but we are greatly released in 2 Peter 1.

We often think that the Lord wants us to abhor ourselves and to forsake everything by our own strength. We may tell ourselves, "I want to be a Christian, I want to abhor myself, and I want to forsake myself." However, everything that the "I" wants is from the self, and ultimately, we are unable to do anything that it wants. The requirements of the Lord Jesus that are shown in the Gospels are fulfilled by the things which relate to life and godliness. All these things have been granted to us by the divine power of God. We may be unable to respond to and to fulfill the requirement in Luke 14, but after we were saved, a life came into us. This life has power and is able to do everything. One significance of salvation is that our sins have been forgiven, but the highest significance of salvation is that we have received the life of God. That we have received the life of God is not a philosophy or a religion but a fact.

We all know that when we repented, confessed our sins, prayed to the Lord, called on His name, believed in Him, and received Him, He became the true and living God to us. He as the life-giving Spirit actually entered into us. This was what transpired in our salvation. Once we were saved, we received the eternal life. The apostle Peter had formerly been a Galilean fisherman. One day the Lord Jesus saw him and told him to let down his nets, and immediately he caught a great number of fish. He was very surprised and amazed at what the Lord had done, and as a result he followed the Lord Jesus (Luke 5:2-11). Later, after he had walked with the Lord outwardly for three and a half years, he saw that the Lord had died, resurrected, and entered into him to be his life. Hence, he gave a testimony in his Epistle, testifying that God's divine power has granted to us all things that relate to life and godliness.

After seeing this light, we will be released. We may jump up and say, "O Lord, I am able to fulfill the requirement in Luke 14, yet it is not I who fulfills it. Rather, You have put the power of Your life into me. You have granted to me the things related to life and godliness. It is not I who fulfills the requirement. Rather, the things that relate to life and godliness are lived out from within me without constraint or hindrance."

Second Peter 1:4 says, "Through which He has granted to us precious and exceedingly great promises that through these you might become partakers of the divine nature, having escaped the corruption which is in the world by lust." God has granted to us precious and exceedingly great promises in order that we may escape the corruption which is in the world by lust. Today the whole world, no matter where you go, is full of corruption. Even though the island of Taiwan is flourishing, is economically prosperous, and has a peaceful and stable living, corruption is everywhere. When a man is in poverty, he only knows to work hard for his livelihood, but once he becomes rich, he begins to do many corrupt and fallen things. How can we escape this kind of trend? Only through the life that God has granted to us inwardly and the promise that God has given to us outwardly can we escape the corruption which is in the world by lust. This is the confirmation of the great promise in Matthew 6:31-33.

SEEKING GOD'S KINGDOM AND GOD'S RIGHTEOUSNESS

The jobs of the working saints are for their livelihood. Whether a man is in a high position or in a low position, whether he eats well or not, he is always busy working for his livelihood. However, we are children of God, and we belong to God. God knows what we need. Then perhaps some people may say, "Since this is the case, does it mean that I do not need to do anything? Maybe I should serve the Lord full-time." We should not think this way. God would never want a slothful person to serve Him. Brother D. L. Moody, a great evangelist in America, once said that he had preached the gospel for several decades and had seen thousands and millions of people get saved, but he never saw a lazy person get saved. Hence, God does not approve of a slothful person. The more diligent a person is, the more God likes him. God takes care of our needs, but He does not want us to be slothful and idle.

Saul of Tarsus was one who greatly persecuted the churches and did away with many believers. One day he obtained from the high priest, who was the highest authority in Judaism, the authority and commission to go to Damascus to bind all those who called on the name of the Lord Jesus. According to the record in the Bible, while he was on the way, a light from heaven beyond the brightness of the sun suddenly shone around him. Then he fell on the ground and heard a voice saying to him, "Saul, Saul, why are you persecuting Me? It is hard for you to kick against the goads" (Acts 26:12-14). In ancient times people used livestock such as a horse or a camel to pull a cart. When the horse or camel was not obedient, the goad, which was yoked to the plow, would subdue the animal. The Lord's word here signifies that Saul had already been yoked to the plow and had no choice but to take the Lord's yoke obediently for the carrying out of the Lord's commission. Once his heart was turned, he was saved. In this way the Lord gained Paul, who was a capable one. He does not want sloth-ful ones.

God is responsible for us, but we must do our part. Human life needs to be supported by food, clothing, housing, and transportation that it may be sustained to fulfill God's pur-pose. Therefore, the Lord promised us that we do not need to be anxious about what to eat or what to drink. Rather, we only need to fulfill our duty to work and to make a living, although we should not pursue after the world and follow its trend. God will take care of us. We only need to seek His king-dom and His righteousness, which is the church today, and His center, Christ. Then God will add to us all that we need. This is a promise.

ESCAPING THE CORRUPTION
WHICH IS IN THE WORLD BY LUST

When some saints first got saved, they loved the Lord very much and pursued the Lord. Perhaps they were still students at that time. But gradually, after they graduated from school, began to work, got married, and had children, they could not keep up with the church life. Previously both the husband and the wife lived in the church life, consecrating themselves to the Lord and pursuing the Lord, and everything they had was for the Lord. But later they had children, one after another, and their burdens in life increased. So they started to work more in order to increase their income, to raise their standard of living, and to prepare funds for their children's education. It is not wrong for the young people to plan for their futures and to establish their families, but we cannot ignore the fact that often there are many seductive and cor-rupt lusts hidden in their plans for establishing themselves. This is similar to what Peter calls "the corruption which is in the world by lust" (2 Pet. 1:4).

Satan does not snare people all at once. Rather, he seduces man step by step. For instance, suppose you are buying a car. You may first buy a locally manufactured car. Then after two years you may see someone driving a French car, and you may want to buy one as well. Then a few years later you may become dissatisfied with the French car and want to change to a German car. As another example, you may look at your house and think that it is too small and too old. You may think that if you do not buy a new one, you should at least remodel the old one. In this way the lust of the world enters our living little by little until it is hard to go back. This is what we must be alert to, be cautious and careful of, and even escape.

In America we often observe that some couples who are foreign students usually live a simple life at the beginning. But some time later, you may go to their house and find that their life is not simple anymore. The sofa in the living room may have been replaced with a new sofa costing two to three thousand dollars. The kitchen may be wide and bright, and the car in the garage may be the latest model. Where did they get the money from? It came from a bank loan. A few months later, however, they may suddenly lose their jobs, and in less than a week, they may even lose their house because the bank may take away everything. This is very common in America. This is the corruption that is in the world by lust and which is always corrupting people.

Today in this materialistic world there is endless temptation. When man falls into the enjoyment of an endless number of material things, he heaps corruption upon himself. The lust that 2 Peter 1:4 speaks about is the lust of the eyes, the lust of the flesh, and the vainglory of life. If what your eyes see is a nice car, where your body lives is in a gorgeous house, and what you think about in your heart is how to be successful, then eventually you will fall into the corruption of lust. There are two things that enable us to overcome all these temptations: one is the inward life that has been granted to us by God's divine power, and the other is the outward promise that as long as we fulfill our duty, God will add to us whatever we need. When we are students, we should study well, and after we graduate, we should work to support our family and our living and to take care of our children. This is enough. We should not be covetous. All covetous people are pitiful. We should not pursue material things because in that pursuit there may be an insatiable covetousness and the lust to covet. Covetousness leads to many lusts and eventually results in corruption.

PREACHING THE GOSPEL IN ALL PROFESSIONS

The saints who are doctors should not labor for more money. It is also better not to be doctors in the big cities. Rather, the doctors should go to the villages so that they may heal their patients and preach the gospel to them at the same time. This would be very effective and worthwhile. If they would do this, they would be able to save at least one person each day. They may contact twenty to thirty patients each day, and among all these patients there should be a son of peace. If they saved one person each day, they would save thirty in a month and three hundred and sixty-five in a year. If they were to work for thirty years as a doctor, then they would be able to save ten thousand. Then when the Lord Jesus comes back, ten thousand people will be there, welcoming them. What a glory this would be! I hope that the brothers and sisters who are doctors and nurses would fulfill their duties to take care of people's bodies and to serve them. But at the same time I hope that they would also learn to serve the Lord. I hope that whenever they see people, they would talk about the gospel, and whenever they see their patients, they would speak to them something about the gospel. In this way the Lord will remember them. This is a principle that should be applied to the saints in every profession.

A normal Christian living is a life of loving the Lord and having fellowship with the Lord. When we wake up in the morning, the first thing we should do is think about the Lord and call, "O Lord Jesus." Then we may open our Bible and read a few verses. While we are washing ourselves, we may meditate over the verses. If we pray and fellowship with the Lord like this, it will be easy for us to live Christ during the day. Those who are teachers will be able to live Christ while they are teaching, and those who work in the office will be able to live Christ in the office. Those who are doctors will be able to live Christ while they see their patients, and those who are housewives will be able to live Christ while they buy their groceries. Everyone will live Christ. Once we have an opportunity, we will talk about the Lord Jesus and preach the gospel to people. Moreover, we should spend at least one or two evenings each week to go door-knocking to speak the gospel or to have home meetings with the saved ones. If we do this, God will surely bless our living. God will absolutely remember and supply us with all that we need. He will supply what to eat and what to put on.

I have been following the Lord for sixty years. During my fifty-five years of serving the Lord I have met many Christians, and I can testify that I have never seen anyone who loved and pursued the Lord lack food or clothing. Though they did not pursue the world for their children, the majority of them and their children were even blessed by the Lord. For such Christians, God is truly their Father and knows what they need. What they seek after in their living is God's kingdom and God's righteousness. They preach the gospel and live for Christ. Ultimately, they live in peace every day. Even though sometimes they may have difficulties, they are able to give them to the Lord. They only know to trust in the Lord, live to the Lord, live Christ, preach the gospel, and live the church life, and the Lord truly adds to them all that they need.

BEING LIGHT AND SALT

The apostle Paul said, "The love of money is a root of all evils" (1 Tim. 6:10). Many people, because of the love of money, fall into sin and ruin themselves. We need to receive the leading to have a part in the Lord's present move, to live the church life, to preach the gospel, and to never go with the tide of this age. Today in Taiwan competition in all the professions is keen, and everyone wants to make more money to raise their standard of living. They want a bigger house and a better car. We should not condemn this because man should make progress, but we Christians should not forget our source. We are God's children and were chosen by Him. We are different from people in general. We are the true welfare of our society and country. As the salt of the earth we remove the corruption from the trend of the world, and as the light of the world we shine in an age of darkness.

Even though outwardly speaking we should not pursue after the world or make progress in a worldly way, we actually encourage people to pursue education and to obtain doctoral degrees. However, we are not the same as secular people. After secular people obtain a master's degree, they want one or two more doctoral degrees for the purpose of making more money and uplifting their status. This is improper and is incompatible with the nature of a Christian. Because we are proper Christians who live ordinary lives on the earth, our walk is the salt of the earth that eliminates many poisonous elements which corrupt people in society. We are also the light of the world that enlightens many darkened corners in people's hearts. Some people accept bribes and gifts from their companies, but we do not. Some try to act meek and submissive and try to flatter their superiors in order to get promoted, but we live by the Lord. This is what it means to be salt and light.

There is bribery in every nation all over the world, but we Christians do not participate in such illegal behavior. When our colleagues come to us and offer us special privileges or rewards, we say, "Sorry, I am a Christian. I will not expose this matter, but neither will I accept this reward." Once we indicate to them our feeling, they will have a feeling in their conscience. In such a situation we become the salt of the earth, eliminating their corruption while at the same time shining as a lamp and enlightening their hearts. How sweet this is!

BEING IN THE ONE WHO EMPOWERS US

Whatever secular people do, they do in groups. This is in keeping with the trend of the age. Hence, society today needs people like us who not only honor God but also, through the gospel, eliminate the corruption and darkness in society so that our society and nation would benefit. Therefore, we should clearly see before the Lord that we are a different group of people. We are not only different from the unbelievers, but we are also different from the believers in the denominations and in the Catholic Church. We have received many truths, we know and experience the divine life, and every one of us has a sweet history with the Lord. Although we might have fallen into a lukewarm condition because of the environment and all kinds of distressing experiences, we are willing to rise up again to put our Christian life in order and to live a life that follows the Lord according to His word.

If our eyes focus merely on the Lord's demand, then it will be impossible for us to fulfill His demand. Luke 14 is an unbearable burden—we cannot do it and are unable to do it. However, what is demanded in the Gospels is entirely supplied in the Epistles. In Philippians 4:12-13 Paul said, "I know also how to be abased, and I know how to abound; in everything and in all things I have learned the secret both to be filled and to hunger, both to abound and to lack. I am able to do all things in Him who empowers me." If Paul could say this, we can also say this, because the One who was in Paul is also in us today. We have learned the secret and are able to do all things in the One who empowers us at every time and in every place.

THE WORKING SAINTS RECEIVING THE COMMISSION TO ESTABLISH HOME MEETINGS

All the working saints are pillars in the church, and the church needs them. Perhaps they may ask what they should do. First, they need to establish home meetings in the new way. The small group meetings need to be strengthened, and the home meetings also need to be strengthened. In the past we had anywhere from one hundred to five hundred people meeting in a meeting hall. We trained and cultivated some saints to be those who stand on the platform and speak. Hence, for a few decades we did not have much increase in number. History tells us that Christians are very capable of charging forward and propagating. Christians are very capable of opening up new frontiers and territories. Paul was such a one. During his time Paul traveled to the Mediterranean Sea, but sadly, because he was imprisoned in Rome, he could not fulfill his desire to reach Spain. Today in this age of technology with such convenient means of transportation, we have no excuse for not accomplishing anything.

In this small island of Taiwan we have had tens of thousands of saints here for twenty to thirty years, but we still have not fully gospelized Taiwan. We cannot justify ourselves in this matter. This responsibility belongs to every one of us. This time the Lord is leading us to gospelize Taiwan but not by merely training a group of preachers. Rather, our goal is that every saint—whether the elderly saints, the younger saints, the working saints, or the saints who are housewives—would rise up to participate. We will not rely on big meetings or hearing good messages because these cannot do that much. We want to motivate everyone to establish home meetings. However, there is a need for pillars in the home meetings. All the working saints should be such pillars. Therefore, the first thing all of us working saints should do is equip ourselves. Then every week we will either meet in our homes or join the meetings at others' homes. This will be our small group meeting. In our meetings we must share how we lived in Christ, read the Bible, prayed, and fellowshipped with the Lord that week. If we all give ourselves in this way, the meetings will be living, we will be able to bring our friends and relatives to be saved, and the saved ones will remain.

Second, we have to go door-knocking at least once a week. We should start with our friends and relatives. After we have visited our friends and relatives, we should knock on the doors of the surrounding neighbors. As long as we knock on people's doors, people will be saved. After they are saved, we have to go to their homes to establish home meetings with them. In brief, as working saints we are required to do only two things: to go to a small group meeting every week and to speak or pray every time we go to the meeting. However, we should not speak in a lengthy way, nor should we give our history. Another thing is that we have to knock on doors or visit people to establish home meetings once or twice every week. If we do not have enough time, we may knock on doors one week and establish home meetings the next week. We must do this once a week for two hours each time. We should make a vow before the Lord to do these two things: establish small group and home meetings and go door-knocking.

CHAPTER FIVE

KNOWING THE PRESENT AGE

Scripture Reading: John 7:38-39; Acts 1:8; Gal. 2:20; Phil. 1:20-21; Rev. 19:10; 22:2

BEING ONE WHO KNOWS THE AGE

We must be those who know the age. If we truly know the Bible, we will be able to see what kind of age we are in according to the prophecies in the Bible and the world situation today. When I was first saved more than sixty years ago, I loved the Bible very much and studied the Bible diligently. At that time some books concerning prophecy had been published in Europe, so I bought some and read them. There are many prophecies related to the world situation, especially prophecies regarding the Jews, the Middle East, and the Persian Gulf nations. These prophecies speak mainly about two matters. The first matter is the restoration of the Jewish nation, and the second matter is the return of Jerusalem into the hands of the Jews.

Jerusalem fell into the hands of the Babylonian king in 606 B.C. For more than two thousand five hundred years, it was fully possessed by the Gentiles without ever falling back into the hands of the Jews. Six to seven hundred years ago, Jerusalem fell into the hands of the Moslems and was possessed by them. During the Six-day War in 1967 the Israelis defeated tens of thousands of Arabs, a numerically superior enemy, and regained Jerusalem.

THE FOCUS OF THE WORLD SITUATION

If we know the prophecies in the Old Testament, we will see that as the Lord's coming approaches, the focus of the world situation will not be on the countries bordering the Pacific or Atlantic Oceans but on those bordering the tiny Mediterranean Sea. The focus will be especially on the eastern coast of the Mediterranean Sea where petroleum is being produced today. When we read the prophecies over sixty years ago, no one paid attention to the matter of petroleum. But in October of 1973 there was a petroleum crisis in the world because the Middle Eastern countries that were producing petroleum froze the supply. Today the economy of the entire world is controlled by petroleum. Although most of the world's industrial and commercial development is occurring in the countries bordering the Atlantic and Pacific Oceans, the focus of international dispute is in the Middle East because of the matter of oil. Every nation is competing for petroleum for their economic benefit, so the Middle East has become the place where much of the world's wealth has accumulated. Hence, the powerful nations are focusing on the Middle East. Everyone is competing for the place where the wealth is.

No one ever imagined that the Persian Gulf region would be in the kind of situation it is in today. One of the greatest and most powerful naval vessels of the United States, the *U.S.S. Missouri,* will go to the Persian Gulf if needed. Undoubtedly, the unpredictable changes in the Persian Gulf region are highly significant. If this situation continues to develop, no politician in the world will be able to tell how the situation will turn out. However, what is certain is that a climax to the situation in the Middle East is imminent, and once the situation explodes, it will be hard to handle.

In 1918 at the end of World War I, various nations signed a peace treaty, but peace was maintained on the earth for only thirteen years. On September 18, 1931 Japan invaded Bei Da Ying in Shenyang, Manchuria. In 1935 Mussolini, the prime minister of Italy, invaded Ethiopia. A few years later in Germany Hitler instigated war in Europe. Thus, in 1939 World War II broke out. In 1941 Japan attacked Pearl Harbor, causing the United States to declare war on Japan. Therefore, in less than twenty years from the time of the amicable settlement of World War I, another war had broken out. It was not until August of 1945, after the United States dropped two atomic bombs on Japan, that Japan unconditionally surrendered, bringing World War II to an end.

From that day until today, a period of more than forty years, there have been no international wars because no one has dared to initiate war. Even if there have been some wars, they have been scattered. With the invention of atomic weapons in this new age, the consequences of an international war breaking out are unimaginable. Hence, most nations dare not initiate a war. However, the Bible clearly says that wars will get fiercer until the world is unable to handle them. Then our Lord will come back.

After World War I the League of Nations was established, but it did not help to maintain a peaceful world situation. Twenty years later World War II broke out. This war involved more nations and was even fiercer. The United Nations was established after this war, but during the past forty or more years, it has not borne much responsibility. The problem of the world situation is very complicated and confused, and no one can solve it.

THE WORLD SITUATION BEING VERY CRITICAL

Due to the two world wars, people have learned not to wage wars, but when the time comes, they will still have to fight. I dare not say that this will happen today, but all those who understand the world situation know that world war is imminent. The Persian Gulf region in particular is like a fuse. Apparently, the entire world situation is stable, but actually, it is very dangerous. Two hundred years ago nations were able to tend to their own business, but today the whole world is connected together. If there is warfare in the Persian Gulf, it will be impossible for other places to be unaffected. The issue of oil will hinder industry, causing economies to collapse. Ultimately, the entire world will be unable to escape this catastrophe.

People from the Moslem countries are generally the descendants of Ishmael. In a prophecy in the Bible, Ishmael is likened to a wild donkey running around crazily, having no regard for its own life, being impossible to tame, and being very unreasonable (Gen. 16:11-12). Today Iran is the same. As a nation it has no regard for its own life. In addition, Soviet Russia may be plotting behind the scenes. Revelation 16 speaks of three unclean spirits as frogs going forth into the whole inhabited earth to stir up wars (vv. 13-14). Behind Soviet Russia is a spirit that never does anything good but instead does evil things, stirring up the world into chaos. Ezekiel 38 and Revelation 20 both speak of Gog and Magog, which, as most Bible expositors acknowledge, refer to Russia and are in the northernmost part of Asia. Rosh and Meshech in Ezekiel 38 correspond with Russia and Moscow (cf. Rev. 20:8, note 1). After the millennium Satan will instigate mankind's last rebellion against God, and Gog and Magog will take the lead. This is a cursed place where man rebels and opposes God. The situation in the Persian Gulf today was stirred up by Soviet Russia. If Soviet Russia had not played a role behind the scenes, there would not have been such a situation in the Persian Gulf today. This is the world situation.

KNOWING THE AGE OF CHRISTIANITY

On the other hand, we also need to know the age of Christianity. Today Christianity is almost in a state of dormancy. The condition of Christianity is like the condition of the church in Sardis in Revelation 3—she has a name that indicates that she is living, and yet she is dead. Everything of Sardis is not living but dead and dying, like a sick person who is about to die. We may also be in a condition like that of Christianity.

In recent years, according to statistics from Christian groups all over the world, there has been a gradual decline in the number of Christians. In the last century it can be said that England took the leading role in Christianity and was the most prominent place for Christianity. Not only were there groups of great teachers in England, there were also many publications. However, in less than one hundred years, Great Britain, especially Northern Scotland, has almost become like a Gentile world of unbelievers. Many people do not even know the name of the Lord Jesus. Although Christianity is the state religion of England, the number of Christians there is decreasing drastically. What is the reason? The reason is that the methods and actions in Christianity are wrong.

Around one hundred and fifty years ago, the Presbyterian Church of Scotland came to Taiwan and established the Presbyterian Church. Now over a hundred years have passed, yet the number of people in the entire Presbyterian Church is only 150,000. A few years ago we obtained statistics on the Christian groups in Taiwan with the greatest numbers of people. First was the Presbyterian Church, which had 120,000 to 130,000 believers at the time. The local churches were the next largest with 70,000 to 80,000. Third was the True Jesus Church with 20,000 to 30,000. The total number of Christians on the entire island of Taiwan was less than 500,000. In other words, the percentage of Christians in Taiwan was less than 2.5 percent of an approximate population of 20 million people. For every one hundred people, there were two and a half Christians at the most. However, in South Korea there are ten million Christians among a total population of fifty million, representing twenty percent of the population. Even in mainland China, where the Communist party persecutes Christians severely, there has been an increase in the number of Christians. Thirty-eight years ago when we left the mainland, the number of Christians plus Catholics was under four million, but now the number of Christians in mainland China is over fifty million—a thirteenfold increase.

The Lord Himself raised up the young people in China to preach the gospel, and the Communist party could not stop them. During the first twenty years that the Communist party was in power, the number of Christians did not increase. It was not until 1970 that the situation greatly changed. Young people rose up to believe in the Lord. They did not have any denominations, missionaries, or pastors. Rather, they all rose up to preach the gospel house by house. Like a flood, in less than twenty years the number of Christians rose from three or five million to fifty million. On the contrary, in Taiwan we have freedom of speech, and our government assists us in every way, providing all kinds of conveniences for the church—the conveniences of transportation, education, and economical development. However, Christianity has not developed much here. Twenty years ago the number of saints among us had already reached today's number. More than one hundred thousand people were baptized, of which tens of thousands met regularly. However, today, twenty years later, we have not had any increase in terms of the total number of saints. We preach the gospel and baptize people year after year, but according to the statistics, there is no increase. This is our failure.

NEEDING TO RISE UP
AND SWITCH TO THE NEW WAY

We all love the Lord and are willing to change the system to evangelize Taiwan, but we need to be clear concerning the entire world situation and the situation of the churches so that we know where we are. Otherwise, we will be like the secular people whose eyes are darkened and who know only to walk but do not know where they are going. We have the prophecy of the Scriptures as a lamp to our feet and a light to our path, and we can testify that we are not groping in the dark (Psa. 119:105). We all know that one day the world will pass away, and our Lord will come back. However, are we ready? We all have to say from our conscience with fear and trembling, "No, we are not ready yet." Then when He comes back, what kind of an account will we give to Him? Time is short. The situations of the world and of the churches are set before us, so we must rise up to change to the new way and to never go back to the old way.

Today there are over forty countries on the earth in which there are churches in the Lord's recovery, and the number of churches is over nine hundred. Among these churches the most stable, experienced, and consecrated is the church in Taipei. For example, recently we decided to purchase land for the building of a meeting hall. We allowed the saints to offer voluntarily according to the Lord's leading through announcements, fellowship, and encouragement. The saints in Taipei and the churches in Taiwan offered 180 million NT dollars within only two months. This shows that the saints truly love the Lord. Since this is the case, we all should rise up quickly to take the Lord's present way—"walking two days' journey in one day" and proceeding forward in a speedy way.

NEEDING TO DEVELOP, EXPLORE, AND MULTIPLY

The way of meeting in the old system was to gather one hundred to three hundred people in a meeting hall every Lord's Day to have a meeting where one person spoke and everyone else listened. This way was practiced for nearly forty years and was very effective during the first five or six years, because at that time we also had small group meetings. During that time the number of saints increased dramatically. In five or six years the number increased a hundredfold, from several hundred to tens of thousands. Later, the saints gradually stopped attending the small group meetings. By 1984 all the small groups had vanished without a trace, and only the big meetings remained. Everyone came to the meeting to hear a message, and of course, the messages were good and profitable. Thus, everyone was edified to love the Lord and to go on. There is no doubt about this. However, from the aspect of development, exploration, and multiplication, we had stopped. Our "family" was good in every way except for the fact that we did not bear children and had no multiplication.

In these thirty years we have been continually meeting and preaching the gospel, and the number of people who have been baptized has been increasing all the time, yet the total number of saints has been decreasing. Taiwan is a small island. From the north end to the south end it is less than five hundred kilometers long. Moreover, transportation is convenient, and the population is dense, making it very convenient for the preaching of the gospel. This is aside from the fact that twenty-five years ago the number of people in the church in Taipei alone had already exceeded twenty thousand, of which several thousand met regularly. Having had this foundation for eight or ten years, we should have preached the gospel all over Taiwan by now. However, until today we have not gospelized Taiwan. We cannot give any excuses for this or justify ourselves.

We must deeply understand that the condition of the churches in Taiwan greatly affects the overseas churches. If the churches in Taiwan do not change their system and make a turn, in the long run several hundred churches overseas will be affected. Hence, we feel that this is a very critical moment, and we must change the system. This is a duty-bound task that requires our absolute devotion. When I look at the semi-dormant condition of the churches all over the earth, this makes me anxious. The condition of the churches in Taiwan truly affects the overseas churches. One example is the churches in the United States. When we first began the work there, the annual rate of increase was over twenty percent, but in recent years it has dropped to less than three percent. Therefore, Taiwan has to change and turn the system around.

SUFFERING LOSS FOR THE OFFSPRING BEING WORTHWHILE

We particularly need to apologize to the elderly saints because old people like to stick to their old habits. To ask them to change their habits is like asking for their lives. We have not visited them one by one to ask for their permission before changing their habits. We truly owe them a lot. However, we still have not completely abandoned the big meetings. According to what we have seen and felt, we should abandon the big meetings so that everyone would then meet in the homes. However, we are not willing to do this because we feel that the elderly saints have been in the church for many years, loving the Lord and the church faithfully. Thus, if we stopped all the big meetings completely, they may not be able to take it all at once. Regardless, the reason for the change is so that our big family would have offspring and children. Then the Lord's recovery would have a future.

One day we all will see our children, grandchildren, and descendants filling the entire earth. At that time we all will exult with joy. The elderly saints may say, "Yes, we like this, but please do not change the way we eat." They may be accustomed to using "chopsticks," but now they must not only continue to use chopsticks but also begin to use "forks." I hope that all the elderly saints would see that we are not condemning the big meeting, saying that it is good for nothing. Actually, a big meeting has its advantages, but it is not easy to produce offspring in a big meeting. By changing our way, our original method, we may bear offspring and be fruitful and multiply.

The Bible tells us that the tree of life bears fruit each month (Rev. 22:2). In the Lord's recovery the truth that we have is clear, and the life that we have is rich. Therefore, in principle we should bear clusters of fruit. Although it should not be difficult to bring one person to salvation each month, this has not been the fact. Therefore, we must come to a critical juncture at which point we must change the system. For a family to prosper and expand, the prerequisite is that this family needs to have many offspring. It needs to bear and rear many children so that many will live. In this way, the family will spontaneously have a bright future. For the sake of the offspring and the future of the entire family, it is worthwhile even if the elderly saints suffer some loss.

THE LIVING OF THE NEW WAY

Having Morning Revival to Enjoy the Lord Every Day

The first thing we should do in our living is to get up early in the morning to call, "O Lord Jesus" and to enjoy two verses. Using these verses we may pray-read the Lord's word and fellowship with the Lord.

Living Christ Every Day

Second, we should live Christ every day. Because we live on the earth and have received the Lord's salvation, we should be a testimony for the Lord. We should be a testimony for the Lord not only with our mouths but also in our living. The furnishings of our home should be elegant and proper, and our clothing should also be noble and graceful, neither luxurious nor too plain. Since we love the Lord, experience that He is true and living, and know that one day He will come back and that we will see Him, we should live Him in our lives and live out a genuine testimony of Him.

As we live in the communities, people are observing our condition. They pay attention to our comings and goings, our attire, and our adornment. If people are fashionable and love the world and we are the same as they, they may not regard us highly. On the contrary, suppose that they are fashionable but we are not and that they adorn themselves but we do not. Then when they encounter difficulties and want to commit an important matter to someone, they will first think of us, because they will clearly know in their hearts who the most proper and reliable people are. This should be our testimony. Thus, not only should we preach the gospel by door-knocking, we should also live out a testimony before our neighbors in our family life, in our comings and goings, in our speaking and attitude, and in our clothing, attire, and adornment. We should be a testimony for the Lord Jesus. We should be such ones.

If we have a proper living in this way, we will not need to do good deeds to benefit mankind, because our living in itself will be a benefit to society. Revelation 22:2 says, "And on this side and on that side of the river was the tree of life, producing twelve fruits, yielding its fruit each month; and the leaves of the tree are for the healing of the nations." The fruit of the tree of life is for food, and its leaves are for the healing of the nations. In the Bible leaves denote man's behavior, that is, his Christian behavior. Good behavior can heal man's corruption. If there are three households of saints living in an apartment building, and they come and go in a proper and modest manner, this will affect everyone in the apartment building. Such a testimony would be very helpful for the preaching of the gospel.

Knocking on Doors to Preach the Gospel and Everyone Speaking in the Home Meetings

Third, if we want to preach the gospel and to preach the Lord Jesus, we need to be ready in season and out of season (2 Tim. 4:2). Some saints are already retired, so they can preach the gospel to their neighbors every day. We do not need to leave the apartment buildings in which we live. As long as we have time, we can knock on doors every day, and gradually the neighbors will know that we are their neighbors and will welcome us. When people open their doors for us, we should preach the Lord Jesus to them. The Lord Jesus should always be our topic. Today the "fish" are numerous, so we not only need to fish with a single line but also with a net. Sometimes, the fish may be so numerous that we ourselves may have to jump into the net. Hence, we should be more diligent in preaching the gospel.

Once a person believes in the Lord and receives the Lord, we should baptize him and go to his home to have home meetings with him. In the home meetings we should not wait for the leading brother to speak a message. Rather, every saint should speak. Unlike the past, we cannot remain silent, looking at one another and waiting for the leading one to speak. In the new way we all should practice preaching the gospel by door-knocking, leading the home meetings, and speaking in the meetings. If we all practice this way, I believe we all will bear new fruit each month and bring people to salvation. Once a person is saved, he is like a child that we have given birth to, and we need to take care of him and nourish him so that he may grow gradually. In this way the church will have offspring.

CHAPTER SIX

THE LIVING FOR THE ESTABLISHING OF PROPAGATION GROUPS

Scripture Reading: Matt. 5:20, 48; Phil. 3:8-10, 12-14; 4:13

The saints who are teachers are all burning in spirit after three days of training and feel that their attendance at the training has been very beneficial. However, the working saints in general may not have the time to join this kind of training. Hence, for those who are not able to join the training, there is a convenient way that will enable them to be part of the propagation and increase of the church. This way is through the establishing of different kinds of propagation groups.

ESTABLISHING DIFFERENT KINDS OF PROPAGATION GROUPS

If you are a housewife, you may establish a housewives' propagation group with the ones in your family as its members. If you are working, you may establish a working saints' propagation group, or if you are a teacher, you may establish a teachers' propagation group. If you are a student, you may establish a young people's propagation group, or if you are a full-timer, you may establish a full-timers' propagation group. Thus, no matter what career, profession, or status you have, you may establish your own propagation group with the brothers and sisters around you. I hope that the brothers and sisters would be able to function organically in different kinds of propagation groups to propagate life.

Three years ago when we changed the system in Taipei, the first thing we did was to shift our attention from big meetings to small group meetings. In one of our meetings when everyone was burning, we declared, "Heaven may fade, and earth may flee, but small group meetings must never be missed." At that time all the saints responded favorably to this change. However, after observing the present situation three years later, we have found that almost none of the saints go to the small group meetings. This is truly pitiful. Therefore, now we need to begin the groups again in a way so that our small groups would not be something arranged or divided according to districts. Rather, they would be something spontaneous—whoever wants to meet in a small group would come together. The small group meeting must be something spontaneous.

PROPAGATING IN THE SMALL GROUP MEETINGS

We all know that the hardest thing regarding the changing of the system is the establishment of the small group meetings. Because we have been influenced by the traditions of Christianity for many years, we emphasize the big meetings, and many people have already formed a habit of not speaking in the meetings. Once this habit of not speaking is cultivated in the saints, it is hard for them to open their mouths again. Therefore, everyone relies on the speaking brothers. When the small group meetings were first established three years ago, the condition of the groups was very good. Every hall decided who should go to which group according to the division of districts on the map and according to the information cards that the saints had filled out. At that time there were four hundred small groups in Taipei with close to four thousand people. We stressed again and again that no one should be the head in the small group meeting but that everyone should speak. Ultimately, however, no one took the lead, and no one spoke in the meetings. Gradually, no one wanted to go to the small group meetings. Starting from today, we should allow the saints to freely choose which group to be in. If someone thinks that the small group meeting that he attends is good and he is willing to continue there, then we should not stop him. But if someone thinks that the small group meeting that he attends is not good and he does not want to go, we should not force him to go there. No matter what way we choose, we must see the importance of the small group meetings.

One brother said that whenever he hears the word *meeting,* his heart sinks, but whenever we talk about propagation, his spirit becomes buoyant and enlivened. Thus, when we go to a small group meeting, we should not say that we are "going to a meeting." Rather, we should say that we are "going to propagate." Our small group meetings are for propagation. Suppose there is a brothers' house that has twelve brothers. These twelve brothers do not need to keep every single regular meeting in the brothers' house. Instead, they may be divided into three to four propagation groups, propagating gradually from the brothers' house to the outside.

I hope that we all would say amen to these suggestions regarding the propagation groups and would carry out the groups accordingly. We all should spontaneously establish various propagation groups and actively propagate life. May we all pray, "O Lord, may You bless us and our fellowship. We truly believe that this is Your work. We ask You to burn our entire being. You are a consuming fire. We ask You to burn us so that we would be neither cold nor lukewarm but that we would all be burning and boiling hot. O Lord, visit us and hear our prayer."

CHAPTER SEVEN

THE FEAST OF GOSPEL LIVING
AND THE RECOVERY
OF THE CHURCH MEETINGS

Scripture Reading: 1 Tim. 3:15-16

THE SUCCESS OF THE EXPERIMENT OF PREACHING
THE GOSPEL THROUGH DOOR-KNOCKING

As we began to change the system, we came back to the Bible and studied and researched the way to meet as it was in the beginning. In a sense, we entered a laboratory where we learned while we experimented. At that time we even increased the number of elders in the church in Taipei from six or seven to over eighty, hoping that the young elders who were in their thirties could help in our study. From the second half of 1986 to this fall, we have had three terms of formal training. About eight to nine hundred saints have joined the training, including saints from Europe, Africa, South America, Central America, North America, and Australia. Including the local trainees, the total number of trainees exceeds five thousand.

In the training the most successful experiment, which succeeded beyond what we had asked or thought, was the preaching of the gospel through door-knocking, bringing people to believe in the Lord and to be baptized. There are currently already over twenty-eight thousand who have been baptized through our door-knocking. This practice has been brought back by the trainees to various places including Europe, Africa, South America, Central America, North America, and Australia and has been very successful. The summer training in the United States last June was changed to a training for the carrying out of the new way with fifteen hundred to sixteen hundred saints in attendance. They were trained in the morning, went door-knocking in the evening, then came back for evaluations and corrections the afternoon of the next day. It was in this way that they baptized thirty-seven hundred people in ten days. This surprised the churches in the United States and Canada, because there were some who had criticized preaching the gospel through door-knocking, saying that although it might have worked in Taiwan, it probably would not work among the Caucasians and people of other colors in the West. No one ever thought that the number of people brought to salvation through the practice of door-knocking in the United States would be comparatively higher than the number in Taiwan.

After the summer training, about five hundred saints from the eastern and western coasts of the United States joined the "door-knocking feast" and eventually baptized 1,019 people. Then we received a letter from Brazil saying that since they have been practicing the new way, the number of churches has increased from 100 to 168. At the same time, about ten churches outside of Brazil, in countries such as Paraguay, Uruguay, and Chile, have been practicing door-knocking from January to September, and the number of baptisms has already exceeded ten thousand. Moreover, we also received a letter from Ghana, Africa saying that some of the saints went to the new cities to preach the gospel by door-knocking and have gained around five hundred people in a short time. Liberia also sent us a cable telling us that they had knocked on 218 doors, and as a result 146 people were baptized.

The first step of preaching the gospel through door-knocking was successful in Taiwan, and the following steps in America and Africa were also successful. But some people still hold a "wait-and-see" attitude, saying that door-knocking will not work in Europe, especially in Scandinavia, Germany, Switzerland, and Denmark. Actually, there was a door-knocking feast in Neuchatel, Switzerland about three weeks ago. Not many went out, but they baptized over a hundred people in two to three days. It did not matter what the race or nationality of the saints was. When we heard the situation of the saints in over nine hundred churches on the six continents of the globe, we truly felt joyful and comforted. The Lord loves His recovery very much.

THE RECOVERY OF THE CHURCH MEETINGS

The greatest difference between the old and the new systems is that the old system focuses on one person speaking and everyone else listening in the big meeting on Lord's Day morning. This matter is obviously not scriptural. In practicality and in the long run, it has not fed the Lord's Body. The purpose of the change of system is to put aside the aspects of the old system completely. The first one in our midst who took this way and brought this recovery and the light of this recovery to us was Brother Watchman Nee. In 1922 when he was in Foochow, Fukien in China, he first began the church meetings. It was in 1932 when Brother Nee came to visit Chefoo that we began the first church meeting in north China in my house. In 1933 I was called to drop my career, and Brother Nee arranged for me to go to Shanghai.

One day he said to me that there was one matter that we should change but that it would be very hard to change. That matter was our way of meeting. He said that all of Christianity focuses on the big meeting on the Lord's Day in which one person speaks and everyone else listens. Brother Nee said that this practice is not biblical and causes many troubles. Thus, it should be changed. Then four years later Brother Nee summoned an urgent co-workers' meeting in Shanghai, mentioning that the system of having a big meeting on the Lord's Day should be changed. The content of the messages of that meeting was published in *The Normal Christian Church Life*. Then eleven years later, when he led the summer training in Kuling Mountain, Fukien, he spoke about this matter twice, and those messages were collected in the book *Church Affairs*.

The change of system has already progressed from the stage of study to the stage of practice. We feel that we have the responsibility to give the saints a clear explanation. When we read *The Normal Christian Church Life* and *Church Affairs,* we felt that we were not worthy to be Brother Nee's co-workers, because his speaking was stronger and more serious than ours. He told us that the Lord's Day message meeting had to be abolished. His speaking was absolute whereas our speaking was general and compromising (*The Normal Christian Church Life,* pp. 175-178).

Brother Nee said that there were two reasons why it would be difficult to abolish the Lord's Day message meeting—because we tend to follow what the nations do (Lev. 20:23; 2 Kings 17:7-8) and because we have nothing to replace it. The outward problem related to abolishing the Lord's Day message meeting is that the brothers and sisters desire to listen to messages, and the inward problem is that the brothers and sisters have a habit of listening to messages (*Church Affairs,* pp. 61-64, 74-77).

ALL THE SAINTS BEING REVIVED IN THE NEW SYSTEM

The church in Taipei will have a big gospel feast. This time our focus will not be on getting a number of people saved but on kindling all the saints in Taipei so that in the new system all the saints in Taipei would be revived and would speak for the Lord in the meetings. In order for the saints to be revived, they need to be filled with the Holy Spirit. It is not too difficult to be filled with the Holy Spirit. Once we get up in the morning, we should call on the Lord's name, talk to Him, and read two verses of the Bible. Then we will live Christ every day. In this way we will be filled with the Holy Spirit. Because we will be living in our spirit throughout the day, surely we will want to meet with our family and have small group meetings with the saints nearby in the evening. Because we will be filled with the Holy Spirit, we will definitely open our mouths in the meeting, and living water will flow out from us. If everyone speaks in the meeting, if I live this kind of living, and if you also live this kind of living, then the meetings will spontaneously be living and rich.

Chapter Eight

BEING UP-TO-DATE
FOR THE REBUILDING OF THE TEMPLE

Scripture Reading: Luke 2:25-38; Ezra 3:10-13; Lev. 20:23; 2 Kings 17:7-8

FOLLOWING THE PATTERN OF THE AGE

Luke 2:25-38 shows us how the elderly brother Simeon and the elderly sister Anna focused on Christ. Ezra 3:12 says that many of the priests, Levites, and the old men who had seen the first house "wept with a loud voice when the foundation of this house was laid before their eyes," and many others shouted aloud for joy. Everyone had mixed feelings of sorrow and joy. These instances in the Scriptures show us how the elderly saints in the church life should concentrate on the matter concerning the will of God. Today many of us elderly saints have the same feeling as those in Ezra. We feel that it is truly a blessing to see the Lord rebuilding His temple in His recovery.

Luke 2 does not speak concerning the building of the house but concerning the changing of a system. It talks about the change of system from the Old Testament to the New Testament. The elderly Simeon and Anna were faithful ones in the old system of the Old Testament. The Holy Spirit descended upon them, and they were full of grace, but they had not yet been baptized. Through the light in Luke 2, we see that these ones were pioneers of the change in system. In fact, Simeon and Anna came earlier than John the Baptist. Even before John the Baptist was born, the elderly Anna and Simeon were taking the lead to change the system.

Therefore, the first pair of people who took the lead

to change the system from the Old Testament to the New Testament was actually the elderly Simeon and Anna. This is truly something remarkable because frequently old people are conservative and hard to change. However, Simeon was changed, and Anna was also changed. Their praises and blessings were delivered from the Mosaic law. They took Christ as the subject and center of their praises and blessings. Neither of them spoke about the Mosaic law or the messages of the Old Testament. Rather, they spoke on the message of the New Testament. We may say that they were up-to-date. I hope that all of the elderly brothers would be like Simeon and that all of the elderly sisters would be like Anna.

THE CHANGE OF SYSTEM BEING TO RECOVER THE GENUINE BUILDING OF THE TEMPLE OF THE LORD

Fifty years ago Brother Nee gave some fellowship regarding changing the old system in the book called *The Normal Christian Church Life.* I am here to solemnly confess my mistake before you. On the one hand, my work here in Taiwan was begun by the Lord, while on the other hand, it was arranged by Brother Nee. Before the work began in Taiwan, the Lord's recovery already had twenty-seven years of history in mainland China from 1922 to 1949. During that period of over twenty years, I was there and experienced many things. So when I came to Taiwan, I reconsidered all of our situations and methods. Like someone sifting the grain on a farm, I sifted out and eliminated all the impractical and unrealistic methods that we had used in mainland China. However, some time ago I began to have some regrets inwardly that when we started the work in Taiwan in 1949 we did not insist on abolishing the Lord's Day message meeting and did not insist on carrying out what Brother Nee had seen in *The Normal Christian Church Life.*

There are three points in Brother Nee's speaking that are ten times heavier than what I had previously thought. First, he said that there is no need to maintain the Lord's Day message meeting (*Church Affairs,* p. 61). Second, he said that the Lord's Day message meeting is a waste (p. 74). What kind of speaking could be heavier than this? Third, he said that to have the Lord's Day message meeting is to follow the customs of the nations and to do what the nations do (p. 61). When Brother Nee spoke of the nations, he was referring to the various denominations. This was a quotation from the type in the Old Testament of the history of the children of Israel. Leviticus and 2 Kings tell us that God charged His people that when they entered the good land of Canaan and when God gave them the land, they should not walk in the customs of the nations, which He would send away before them (Lev. 20:23; 2 Kings 17:7-8).

Those who have a comprehensive view of the Old Testament know that these customs refer to the nations' worship of idols in the land of Canaan, their free worship of the pillars, Asherahs, and the idols of their gods in high places as spoken of in Deuteronomy 12. However, God said to the children of Israel that they should not follow the customs of the land. Rather, "the place which Jehovah your God will choose out of all your tribes to put His name, to His habitation, shall you seek, and there shall you go" (v. 5). God wanted the children of Israel to go to the place that He chose to build a dwelling place, a temple, for His name and to worship Him there three times a year. Later the children of Israel fell, and they followed the customs of the nations to worship God not in the temple but in various high places. When they worshipped God, they did so in the same way the nations worshipped the demons. Thus, they followed the customs of the nations.

In the same way, when God raised up the church in the age of the New Testament, He indicated clearly in the New Testament that the church should be sanctified and should never follow any custom or become worldly. However, in the two thousand years of Christian history, because of the degradation of the church, the church has deviated in many matters, especially in the matter of the Lord's Day service and worship. The church has deviated from what God ordained in the New Testament—to worship Him in a way that is not under the influence of the world. Once God's people deviated from the God-ordained, unique way of worship, they fell into the Gentiles' way of meeting. They gathered the related people at a certain time, and one person spoke while everyone else listened.

About sixty years ago in 1922 God raised up His recovery in China. Brother Nee was there leading the first meeting. At that time he had not yet seen the proper way to meet, so we naturally followed the way of Christianity. We practiced meeting in this way for as long as eleven years. In 1933 I was called by the Lord to leave my job and went to see Brother Nee in Shanghai. At that time as I was with Brother Nee, he mentioned to me this matter of the Lord's Day service, feeling that it was neither biblical nor pleasing to God, but that it was actually following the custom of the denominations. More than fifty years ago the Lord showed us this mistake, but we have not begun to eliminate this mistake until now. Brother Nee said that it would not be easy to overthrow this tradition because it would require everyone to overthrow it together. Through the light in the book of Ezra, we see that to change the system is actually to recover the genuine building of the temple of the Lord.

THE TRADITIONAL MESSAGE MEETING NULLIFYING MAN'S SPIRITUAL FUNCTION

The New Testament tells us that as saved ones we have been regenerated in our spirit and that from the time we were saved, God has been edifying and building up our spirit. Ephesians 2:22 clearly reveals that our spirit is God's dwelling place in us. Hence, to build up our spirit, the individual spirit, is to build up God's dwelling place, God's temple. On the other hand, the church is also God's house and God's temple. But how do we build up the church? It is through all the saved ones encouraging one another and functioning in mutuality according to their fellowship with the Lord and the experiences of life they have had with the Lord in their spirit. The Body of Christ is built up through the spiritual development of all the members. Today in Christianity and even among us, the message meeting on Lord's Day morning is a gathering where one person speaks and everyone else listens. Apparently, the meeting is for bringing people to the Lord. To bring people to the Lord is quite good; however, after a person has believed in the Lord and has been baptized, this practice of one person speaking and everyone else listening immediately nullifies his function. His spiritual function is annulled. There is no need for him to preach the gospel, to pray, or even to serve, because there are already some who can do these things properly. All he needs to do is to come to the Lord's Day service in the morning and listen to the message.

Many of us can testify that when we were first saved, we were inwardly touched very much and were full of zeal. We not only wanted to testify to other people but also wanted to preach the gospel to them. However, when we came to the Lord's Day meeting, we were not required to say anything. The longer we attended this kind of meeting, the more we forgot how to speak. After meeting for a month, half a year, or a year, we did not speak at all. Therefore, Brother Nee said that this kind of Lord's Day meeting in which one person speaks and everyone else listens is very deadening.

The result of people being deadened is that their spiritual function is completely nullified, and ultimately, there is no building up. The translators of the Chinese Union Version rendered the phrase *building up* in 1 Corinthians 14 as *edification* (vv. 3-5), but in Greek this phrase can mean either edification or building up. As a rule, the word *edification* should be rendered as *building up*. Today is there any building up in the Catholic masses, the Protestant services, or our Lord's Day meetings? Strictly speaking, these kinds of meetings do not build up the church that much. Brother Nee even said in a message that we should tell the newly saved ones that when they attend the Lord's Day meeting, they are not coming to a meeting of the church but to a meeting of the work. If we have been attending the Lord's Day meeting for thirty years and there still has not been the building up of the church, then our situation is truly pitiful.

Earlier we mentioned that Brother Nee spoke some words concerning the Lord's Day meeting in *The Normal Christian Church Life* and *Church Affairs,* but we never emphasized them in our speaking to the saints. Having clearly read these words again, we have been truly enlightened within, and we realize that these words are very serious. Fifty years ago

Brother Nee pointed out that we do not need to maintain the Lord's Day message meeting, but we completely forgot this word. When I came to Taiwan thirty-eight years ago in 1949, I should not have maintained the Lord's Day message meeting, yet I continued it. I have always regretted this. Similarly, when I started my work in the United States more than twenty years ago, I did not change this practice.

DEVOTING OURSELVES TO CHANGING THE SYSTEM

From 1976 to 1977 the Lord showed me that He had taken away the blessing. Although the number of churches in every place was increasing, from 1977 there was almost no increase in the number of saints, especially in Anaheim. There had not been any increase for one year, two years, and even three years. Everyone seemed to be very busy every day and were also baptizing people, but when we counted the total number of saints, we found that it had not increased but decreased over the years. When I left Anaheim in 1984, the number of saints there was less than that of ten years ago.

It is the same with the work in Taiwan. For example, consider the church in Taipei. Seemingly, all the saints are very busy. Sometimes they baptize dozens of people, and sometimes they baptize several hundred people, but after these people are baptized, we do not know where they go. This may be likened to someone who has a business. He may be very busy every week and apparently may have a very good and promising business, but at the annual accounting time he discovers that his gross assets two years ago were $35 million, but after a year of operation his gross assets had been reduced to $34 million, and after another year of operation, they have been reduced to $33 million. We all can see the result. Therefore, I came to an end and did not know how to continue the work. But at that time I was awakened to remember what Brother Nee had said fifty years ago concerning not maintaining the Lord's Day message meeting and concerning the Lord's Day message meeting being a waste. After much consideration, I felt that if I wanted to deal with this problem, I would have to go back to Taipei. Taipei is a base for the overseas development of the Lord's recovery, and if we do not clear up this matter in Taipei, there will be no way to do it elsewhere.

This time I came back with a determined will and a mind to devote myself to this problem at any cost. My wife reminded me again and again that I am already over eighty years old. Every time I heard this word, I looked to the Lord inwardly, saying, "O Lord, You have heard all these things, and You also know that my life and death are in Your hand. If You want me to live for several more years or even ten more years, it is not impossible. No matter what, as long as I have breath, I am willing to devote myself to do what I should do."

The work here in Taiwan was started by me. The meeting halls here, especially the main meeting halls such as Hall One, Hall Three, and Hall Four in Taipei, as well as Hall One in Kaohsiung, were purchased mostly by my ministry. When we first came to Taiwan, all of us were very pressed financially and were unable to offer anything for the purchase of the meeting halls. In 1958 I went to Southeast Asia and labored there for a few months. There was a brother who asked me to tell him all the financial needs for the work in Taiwan, because the Lord had given him a burden to bear the entire cost for the Lord's work in Taiwan, no matter how much it was. So when I came back to Taiwan, I began to build meeting halls, and I took care of the monthly living expenses of over one hundred and twenty full-time co-workers.

Please forgive me for saying this. Although I cannot be compared to Paul, allow me to imitate him in his speaking to the churches. To the churches in Taiwan, I am like an old father. Hence, I do not have any concerns in coming back to change the system. Some time ago I was led by the Lord to read one of Brother Nee's books to you, and after reading it, we all had the assurance that we needed to change the system. To change the system is not mainly to change our way of meeting but to bring the church back to her condition before the degradation.

CHRISTIAN MEETINGS BEING
FOR THE BUILDING UP OF THE BODY OF CHRIST

On the day of Pentecost three thousand people were saved.

After they were saved, they had meetings at various homes, and they all spoke. They were filled with the Holy Spirit, and they immediately began to speak. We all have had this kind of experience—the more we are filled with the Holy Spirit, the more we speak, and the more we speak, the more we are filled with the Holy Spirit. This kind of gathering builds up our spirit and the spirits of other people. Hence, in the Epistles Paul said that in the Christian meetings there should be mutuality (1 Cor. 14:26-27, 29). There should not be only one person speaking while everyone else listens. Rather, the meetings should be mutual. You build me up, and I build you up—this is the building up of the Body of Christ.

Today we cannot see the Body of Christ in Catholicism or Protestantism. Although the light among us is very strong, and we receive much speaking, when we look at the condition of our meetings, we cannot see much of the reality of the Body of Christ. Three hundred people gather here on the Lord's Day, but only one speaking brother functions, and the rest of the people remain silent. There are even some saints who have been meeting with us for several decades, but they have never opened their mouths in the meeting or prayed publicly among us. In this kind of condition we neither have the reality of the Body of Christ nor do we see the Body of Christ. Instead, we only have a religious service.

We see from the history of the beginning of our work in Taiwan that the Lord is rich in mercy. When we first arrived in Taiwan, the brothers and sisters did not have much money, and the church also did not have much money. But in His sovereignty, the Lord sent two overseas Chinese brothers from the Philippines to Taipei to buy half of the land in front of the meeting hall for the church, about one thousand and eighty square feet. Later, the Lord opened the way for me to go to Southeast Asia, and a brother willingly received the burden to take care of the financial need for the work in Taiwan. He did this for a period of ten years. What the Lord did was truly His mercy. However, even though the Lord has blessed us like this, we still keep one thing that is not blessed by the Lord, that is, our Lord's Day meeting in which one person speaks and everyone else listens.

We are fellowshipping this matter with you and particularly with the elderly saints because the elderly saints among us are not only our seniors in age but also have a long and precious history. Through all these years, the Lord has been releasing the truth and supplying life continuously in His recovery, taking care of the saints in life and somewhat perfecting them in the truth. The elderly saints have been in the midst of this precious history of the Lord's recovery. We thank the Lord and treasure this history with the elderly saints.

Today we need to apologize to the elderly saints that in our service to the church we have not followed the light that Brother Nee saw several decades ago regarding changing the Lord's Day message meeting. This was our negligence and mistake, and now we owe something to the Lord and to the elderly saints. Thus, we resolve to put the change into practice. However, we must consider the elderly saints who have been accustomed to meeting in this way now for several decades. If we change the Lord's Day meeting too quickly, we are afraid that according to their feeling the change will not only be an inconvenience but also a cause for sorrow. Once there is no more Lord's Day message meeting, they may have nowhere to go and may not know what to do. Moreover, if they want to bring new ones, they may not know the proper place to bring them to. We have to consider all these matters. When we look at a matter, we cannot and will not merely consider it from one side. So in these three years we have not made it a regulation to completely abolish the Lord's Day message meeting. Rather, when we fellowshipped with the elders, we stressed that we should maintain this meeting in various meeting halls on the Lord's Day morning.

On the other hand, we all have to be clear that many saints have joined the training ever since it began. After passing through the training, they went out door-knocking and brought over twenty-eight thousand people to salvation. Among these baptized ones, around five thousand were brought into the church life. These new ones who are being brought in are not meeting at the meeting halls but in the communities. From this perspective, these three years have not been a waste. This is an increase to the church in Taipei.

Now we have received the Lord's leading to make a resolution with the elders and co-workers to stop the Lord's Day message meetings, but please do not worry. Brother Nee said in the past that we could not abolish the Lord's Day message meeting because we did not have something to replace it. But now after a few years of training and many experiments, we have found that we have a new way to meet, not only for our Lord's Day meeting but even for our other regular meetings. I believe that the elderly brothers and sisters will all welcome the change of system with happiness and joy. With the change of system, our meetings will be based on two matters—first, the building up of the spirits of the saints, and second, the building up of the Body of Christ. These two matters must be implemented by the new way of meeting that we are implementing in changing the system. The meetings in the old system could not build up the church, but the meetings in the new system are directed toward building up the spirits of all the saints and building up the Body of Christ.

THE WAY FOR THE ELDERLY SAINTS TO FUNCTION

I hope that all the elderly saints would see that when we go forward, they will be the most useful people in the Lord's Body. Never think that because you are old, do not have much physical strength, and cannot be very active, that you cannot follow the new system. You must realize that in the new system there are other matters besides door-knocking, which occupies only five percent of the new system. We elderly saints can pray, and we also have spiritual knowledge. We need only to change our habit of not speaking and begin to speak at home and also to our friends and relatives and in the meetings.

After the change in system, our meetings will not regulate who can speak and who cannot speak, and there will be no such thing as the preaching of messages. All the saints will be able to speak and pray in the meetings. If every one of us speaks and prays, the meetings will be living. The more we speak, the more our spirits will be built up, and at the same time, we will build up others. I really hope that we elderly saints would do three things—pray much at home, come to the meetings and pray, and open our mouths to speak at home, to our friends and relatives, and in the meetings. If all of us are willing to do this, the change in system will be successful, the Lord will be full of joy, and we also will be full of joy.

CHAPTER NINE

THE CENTRAL PURPOSE OF GOD'S ECONOMY REGARDING THE MEETINGS OF THE BELIEVERS

The Lord has led us to the focus of the new way and the central point of our change in system, that is, the central purpose of God's economy regarding the meetings of the believers. If we get through in this matter, our change of system will be successful, and the new way will be opened to us. I believe that since the Lord has begun this good work, He will surely complete it. In these few years the Lord's changing of the system among us has been active but not rushed. We have been very cautious and have considered, studied, and experimented in many aspects. We are viewing this change of system from the central point of God's New Testament economy. God has also led us to see in the past few years that this economy, which is the highest revelation, is the focus of the New Testament. There is a central purpose in God's economy, and there must be a means for this central purpose to be accomplished. The means is the meetings of the believers.

KNOWING THE PURPOSE OF THE MEETINGS OF THE BELIEVERS

Christians are those who meet all the time. They have a communal characteristic. They are not like butterflies, which fly individually. Rather, they are like bees, which gather together. Many Christians, however, have been meeting continually for decades and still do not know the purpose of their meetings. Most Christians think that the purpose of going to a meeting is to worship God, to learn the truth, and to receive some spiritual benefit. But according to the revelation of the

Scriptures, the central purpose of the believers' meeting is two-sided. On one side it is to build up the believers in spirit (Rom. 14:19; 15:2; 1 Cor. 14:3), and on the other side it is to build up the Body of Christ in the spirit (1 Cor. 14:4; Eph. 2:22; 4:12, 16). The central point of our change in system and our taking the new way is to carry out this central purpose.

THE BUILDING UP OF THE BELIEVERS IN SPIRIT

The first aspect of the central purpose is to build up the believers in spirit. Here the *spirit* refers to our human spirit. The word *build* is often rendered as *edify* in the Chinese Union Version, but in Greek this word implies building because the root of this word in Greek means "house." When edification is mentioned, people generally do not think of the building of a house. Rather, they think of a person who does not have much education and who needs more education and further study, or they think of someone who is not sensible and who needs some enlightening that he may be edified. Generally, people have a broad understanding of the word *edification*. However, in the Bible *edification* denotes building up.

When we are going to build something, the first thing we need to do is to prepare the materials. Without the materials there cannot be any building. We must first prepare bricks, stones, wood, steel, and cement for the building. Paul said that he had laid the unique foundation and that we must build upon it with proper materials such as gold, silver, and precious stones and not with improper materials such as wood, grass, and stubble (1 Cor. 3:10-12). The first purpose of our meetings is to build up one another. It is not to adjust one another's mistakes, which is merely edification, but to build the gold, silver, and precious stones—the essence of the Triune God—into one another.

Taking the Triune God as the Materials

Gold, silver, and precious stones are the proper materials. Gold signifies the divine nature of the Father with all of its attributes, silver signifies the redeeming Christ with all of the attributes and virtues of His person and work, and precious stones signify the transforming work of the Spirit with all of its attributes. Hence, to build with gold, silver, and precious stones is to build with the Triune God—the Father, the Son, and the Spirit. Suppose that today we heard a message through which the divinity of God the Father as gold, the redeeming element of God the Son as silver, and the transforming element of God the Spirit as precious stones were not built into us. The message we heard would be empty and vain, and we would be built with improper materials such as wood, grass, and stubble. Every time we meet, we must use the proper materials, which are the Father's nature, the Son's redemption, and the Spirit's transformation work as gold, silver, and precious stones, to build up the believers and one another.

In Romans 14:19 Paul told those who were living the church life, "So then let us pursue the things of peace and the things for building up one another." The "things of peace" and "the things for building up" are the things that keep the oneness of the Body of Christ and that minister the Triune God to our fellow members. You may minister the golden nature of the Father into me through the Word, I may minister the silver element of the Lord Jesus in His redemption into you, and another may minister the transforming element of the Spirit as precious stones into us. As a result all of us are mutually built up. For this reason we must maintain the peace. Peace enables us to live the church life together without debating, opinions, quarreling, or murmuring. In this kind of peaceful atmosphere you can minister God to me, I can minister God to you, and everyone can mutually minister the Triune God to one another.

Ministering the Triune God to One Another through Speaking

If we want to minister the Triune God to one another, it must be done by speaking, speaking not ordinary words but the words of the truth. This requires our learning. We may be very capable of speaking funny and humorous things, but when we are asked to speak in the meeting to minister God to others, we may be silent and not know how to speak. This is why we prefer not to speak in the meetings, because once we speak, we expose ourselves. For example, before a person speaks, people may think that he is quite good, but once he speaks, he immediately exposes himself. This is our problem. If everyone sits properly in the meeting and neither prays nor speaks, then of course we must rely on the preacher to speak by himself. However, does this kind of meeting build up others? We may know a few things and may have gold, silver, and precious stones in us, but we may keep all the things that we have gained inside, refusing to take out even one of them. Then where is the building?

From the very beginning when Brother Watchman Nee brought to us the way of the Lord's recovery, he showed us a clear vision that we all have to speak in the meetings. But very few among us have spoken until now. The general situation is that no matter what kind of meeting we have, there is always one person speaking while everyone else listens. Even the so-called fellowship meeting is arranged beforehand. With this kind of situation, how can we build up others in the meetings? In August of 1948 we started our work in Taipei, and during the first few years there was a trend toward an increase in the number of saints. But after 1958 the number stopped increasing, and the meetings were not living. The reason for this was the lack of the spirit. Therefore, in 1960 we began to speak on the exercise of the spirit, the use of the spirit, and the release of the spirit. Then in 1961 we spoke on this more emphatically. At that time very few or perhaps even none of the saints used and exercised their spirit. Then I personally wrote some hymns related to this matter and had everyone sing them. Later I went to the United States and started the work there. The Lord gave me the clear guidance that I had to begin with the spirit. Hence, our beginning in the United States was successful. At that time people were calling on the name of the Lord and pray-reading the Lord's word. These matters are related to the spirit.

However, this produced a side effect. There were some more refined people such as university professors and company managers who, after joining our meeting, said, "We have no way to join your kind of meeting. We who do business or teach are busy for five or six days a week, and on the Lord's Day we want to be more relaxed. We want to go to a quiet chapel to have a Sunday service for relaxation. There they have a choir that sings and a pastor who preaches. Even though we may not understand what the choir sings or what the pastor preaches, these things are not bad and give us peace in our hearts. Your kind of meeting in which you are calling, 'O Lord' and 'Amen' all the time is not quiet. Moreover, you also force me to speak. I am a boss in a company, and if you ask me to stand up to speak and I am not able to do so, I will lose my face. I will not attend your kind of service. Instead, I will go to a tall and magnificent chapel with a quiet atmosphere."

Some who had successful careers in society said, "Today is the age of science, and everything is scientific. Doctors should be scientific doctors, lawyers should be scientific lawyers, and pastors should be scientific pastors. Only those who have learned how to be a pastor should preach in the meetings. It is not scientific to ask us who have never studied theology to speak." Apparently this sounds reasonable, but where is the building? A person who does not believe in Jesus or attend the Sunday service in a chapel looks one way, but after he believes in Jesus and has been attending the Sunday service in a chapel for thirty years still looks the same. Why is this? This is because the Triune God does not have the opportunity to add Himself into him. The Lord's Day meeting in Christianity makes man attend a service but does not add the Triune God into him. Hence, in principle all the meetings in Christianity, including ours, have lost the goal of the meetings, which is to build up the believers with the element of the Triune God.

THE BUILDING UP OF THE BODY OF CHRIST
IN THE SPIRIT

The second aspect of the central purpose of the meetings of the believers is to build up the Body of Christ in the spirit. In the various denominations in Christianity today we almost never hear messages on the building up of the Body of Christ. In the New Testament, however, this matter is mentioned again and again, especially in the Epistles of Paul.

First Corinthians 12 and 14 specifically speak of the building up of the Body of Christ. The subject of Romans 12 is also the building up of the Body of Christ. Ephesians 4 speaks of this matter in an even deeper way. Verses 10 through 11 say that after His ascension Christ received gifts from God and gave them to the church—"And He Himself gave some as apostles and some as prophets and some as evangelists and some as shepherds and teachers, for the perfecting of the saints unto the work of the ministry, unto the building up of the Body of Christ" (vv. 11-12).

Then verse 16 says, "Out from whom all the Body, being joined together and being knit together through every joint of the rich supply and through the operation in the measure of each one part, causes the growth of the Body unto the building up of itself in love." *Out from whom* denotes that all the members are out from Christ the Head. The building up of the Body of Christ is through every joint of the rich supply. These joints are the supplying joints. They have a rich supply and operate in the measure of each one part. Although a nose is small in measure, it has its particular function. While a shoulder is big, it also has its particular measure and function. Through the operation of each one part, all the parts are joined together and knit together. We as members in the Body are being joined and knit together. Once a small part is detached from the Body, it withers and dies. But when the whole Body is joined and knit together, this causes the growth of the Body unto the building up of itself in love. This matter is spoken of and described in the Bible, but it difficult to find such a situation in Christianity and even among us.

Building Requiring Proper Meetings
with Every Believer Speaking

The apostles, while they were still on the earth, thought that it would not be too long before the Body of Christ would be built up and Christ would come back. However, it has been more than one thousand nine hundred years since they passed away, and there is still no trace of the Body of Christ. It seems that the Lord's coming back will not be in the immediate future. On the earth today there are various denominations in Christianity, and there is also the Lord's recovery, but we cannot see the building up of the Body of Christ in any of these groups. For example, in the church in Taipei, the birthplace of the overseas work of the Lord's recovery, we still cannot see much building up of the Body of Christ. What is the reason? The reason is that we do not have proper meetings. In the New Testament the building requires proper meetings, whether they are for the building up of individual members or the building up of the Body of Christ. What is a proper meeting? In brief, a proper meeting is one in which all the believers speak.

In the New Testament we cannot find a single example of a regular church meeting in which one person spoke and everyone else listened. However, there were some irregular meetings in which one person spoke and everyone else listened. For example, Acts 20:7 tells us that after Paul arrived in Troas, the saints gathered together to break bread on the first day of the week. Before they broke the bread, Paul conversed with them until midnight. Subsequently, a young man sank into deep sleep and fell from the window where he was sitting (v. 9). That was a special occasion, a special kind of meeting in which one person spoke and everyone else listened. Then Paul went down and saved the young man's life, and everyone went up to break the bread. It was after midnight that they broke the bread. After they broke the bread, everyone continued conversing and fellowshipping all the way until daybreak, at which time they saw Paul off (vv. 10-11). This was an example of a special meeting.

In the New Testament the regular meetings, whether they were home meetings, small meetings, or big meetings, were not meetings in which only one person spoke. First Corinthians 14 shows us that when the whole church came together for a big meeting, more than one person spoke. Paul said, "Whenever you come together, each one has..." (v. 26). Someone may have had a psalm, someone else may have had a revelation, another one may have had a teaching, still another may have had a tongue, and another one may have had an interpretation. In the meeting each one had something. The meeting was not one in which one person spoke and everyone else listened. Therefore, based on the light of the New Testament, the regular church meetings may sometimes be a coming together of the whole church or sometimes meetings in various homes, but regardless of the difference in size, the principle is that everyone speaks.

Meetings in Which Everyone Speaks Requiring Us to Live an Overcoming Life

A meeting in which one person speaks and everyone else listens is a big relief to all of us because it does not matter whether we quarrel at home every day. As long as we bring our Bible bag to the meeting on the Lord's Day, our conscience will be all right because we do not need to speak. Whether we failed or overcame during the week, we will feel fine as long as we go to the meeting, because in it just one person speaks and everyone else listens. However, a meeting in which everyone speaks requires us to live an overcoming life, to fellowship with the Lord, to walk according to the spirit, to be burning in spirit, to call "O Lord Jesus" all the time, and to speak about Jesus to people every day. Only in this way will we have the word and the spirit, and only in this way will our speaking have content.

I can testify that one who calls "O Lord Jesus" from morning to evening, who walks in the spirit and according to the Spirit, who is burning in spirit, and who speaks Jesus to people will surely look forward to the meeting with anticipation, because once he comes to the meeting, he will be able to share his experience with other saints and fellowship about it. What is a Christian meeting? It is a meeting in which Christians share Christ and speak Christ. A Christian meeting is a meeting in which everyone speaks and in which the content of their speaking concerns their experiences of overcoming, enjoying Christ, and being enlightened.

If we have a small group meeting consisting of twelve people, but eleven of them lose their tempers at home or the husbands and wives condemn each other, then it will be impossible for anyone to speak because our spirits will be like flat tires. However, suppose the saints have family propagation groups at home, and everyone is revived. The husband confesses to his wife, causing her to be enlivened, and the wife also says to her husband, "I am wrong," causing the husband to be opened. Through this kind of mutual confession and forgiving, this family will spontaneously be living. Then when they come to the small group meeting and open their mouths, people will be supplied and edified. I hope that the meetings of more than nine hundred local churches all over the globe would begin with confession in the homes. We need a revival, and we need family propagation groups and other kinds of propagation groups. The change in system is not merely for the purpose of having a change in form or a change in content. Rather, it is for the purpose of causing the dead to be raised and all the saints to be enlivened.

One Person Speaking and Everyone Else Listening Killing the Function of the Believers

In the past we arranged for the co-workers to speak twice a week. Consequently, they neither ate well nor slept well during those two days. But now they have been released because they do not need to give a message on the Lord's Day. The new way of meeting will be beneficial to both the co-workers and the saints and will be a new beginning for them. I say again that we do not want one person speaking and everyone else listening. Instead, we want everyone speaking and everyone listening. We may all say with our mouths, "Yes, this is right. We should have everyone speaking and everyone listening. It is scriptural to have mutuality." However, even those who have been saved for many years and know the Bible do not speak in the meetings. This is a very serious matter that we all must consider.

I say again that based on our observation, the Lord has no way in Christianity. According to the statistics, the number of Christians in the various big or small denominations in the United Kingdom and the United States is diminishing. This has also been the case among us. We did not have a way to go on. When we looked into the reason, we found that it was the way of one person speaking that had killed everyone's function. However, if everyone speaks and is revived, the church will have a way to go on.

Everyone Being Revived to Build Up
the Body of Christ by Taking the New Way

When we went out to knock on doors recently, although we encountered a severe typhoon that caused flooding in Taipei and submerged many places, we all went out in one accord and eventually baptized about seven thousand people. Not only were entire households saved, but also around fourteen hundred home meetings were established. If only one out of ten from these seven thousand baptized ones remains, we will still have around seven hundred people. If we gain only one percent of these fourteen hundred homes, we will still have fourteen homes. This truly fills us with joy. When we went out, we endured the wind and rain and knocked on more than two hundred thousand doors in ten days. This was an unprecedented event among Christians. Moreover, we immediately established home meetings at the homes of the saved ones to teach them the truths and to speak to them from the *Life Lessons*. We truly saw the Lord's blessing and the presence of the Holy Spirit.

Hence, we should be all the more watchful that our spirits would be enlivened. Not only we ourselves have to be living, but we should also enliven others. When we go to a new one's home, we should not speak too much. Rather, we should lead him to open his mouth to pray, confess, deal with his sins, release his spirit, and exercise his spirit. For example, we may teach him to say, "It is so good to believe in Jesus." When he first begins, he may speak only from his throat and not from his spirit, but gradually we can lead him to speak from his spirit. Then we have to lead him to pray, confess, fellowship with the Lord, and be filled with the Spirit. In this way when he comes to the meeting, he will be able to speak by faith and will have the Holy Spirit poured out upon him. According to Acts, once Peter or Paul stood up to speak, the Holy Spirit filled him outwardly.

Furthermore, we have to help them to always be in spirit to follow the spirit, walk according to the spirit, be burning in spirit, open their mouths in the meeting, and speak to people about the gospel. In this way every one of our meetings will build up the believers. They will build up the Body of Christ with the Triune God and build the Triune God into the believers so that they may be joined and knit together. This is to build up the Body of Christ. I hope that we all would receive this burden to practice this so that our spirit would be enlivened and we would daily be filled in spirit, having both the inward and the outward filling. Then we all will be living people, speaking the words of the truth in the meetings and building up others' spirits and the Body of Christ.

CHAPTER TEN

THE WAY TO PRACTICE
THE CHANGE OF SYSTEM

Scripture Reading: Acts 2:46; 5:42; 1 Cor. 14:26; Heb. 10:25; 1 Cor. 14:4, 12

In October 1984 we mentioned the matter of changing the system and taking the new way in Taipei, but we did not change the system immediately because we still had to study the practical steps of the new way. Generally speaking, we should divide the practice of the new way into three steps. The principle of each step is based entirely on the revelation of the New Testament.

THE SWEETNESS AND THE IMPACT OF "THE FEAST"

In 1986 we began to have a formal training in Taipei. We spent all of our energy, finances, manpower, and resources to hold a training in Taipei because among the over nine hundred churches in the six continents, there was no place more suitable than Taipei for carrying out our experiments and training for the new way. At the present time we have held three terms of training, and the total number of trainees, who were from over twenty countries among the six continents, has been over five thousand. Through the studies and experiments we carried out in the training, the Lord is leading us to take an unprecedented new way.

In September of this year in Taipei, we had a large-scale gospel activity called "the feast." This name came from the type in the Old Testament. The children of Israel had to go to Jerusalem three times a year to keep certain feasts, including the Feast of Passover, the Feast of Pentecost, and the Feast of Tabernacles. In the Feast of Tabernacles, after gathering in the produce from their threshing floors and winepresses, the children of Israel gathered before God with their sons and daughters, male and female servants, the Levites, and the sojourners, orphans, and widows who were within their gates to enjoy God and the riches that God had given them. At the same time this allowed God to enjoy His people so that He could be satisfied (Deut. 16:13-17).

We deeply feel that if the churches from a certain district, a certain country, or even several countries would come together at a certain time, as the children of Israel came together to keep the feasts in Jerusalem, the impact of this action would be beyond expectation. The training in Taipei during these few years has gathered saints from various places to labor together, and the result has been very good. In the training in Anaheim there were saints from churches all over the United States and some from overseas who labored together; ultimately, the efficiency of our labor was even greater than it was in Taipei. Therefore, in the long run we feel that all the churches should carry out this activity of "feasting." For example, if a church in a region has the burden to "keep the feast," the church should fellowship this burden with the surrounding churches so that they may carry it out together. In this way they will gain a considerable number of people, and their labor will be more efficient.

DEVELOPING AND STRENGTHENING
THE CARE IN DIFFERENT DISTRICTS

The saints who joined the feast were not only from various places in Taiwan. There were also 617 saints who came from twenty countries all over the world. Prior to the feast, the trainees who had joined the full-time training coordinated with some local saints and went out to preach the gospel by door-knocking. They baptized around twenty-eight thousand people, but due to the shortage of people to take care of and shepherd them, the rate of survival among them was not very high. Therefore, the main focus of our feast this time was not to baptize people but to gain people household by household. Those who went out door-knocking went not only to baptize people and gain them as individuals but to establish home meetings in their homes in order to gain their households, because a person whose entire household is saved is more secure and easier to take care of. By the end of the ten days of the feast, 7,825 people had been baptized and over a thousand homes had home meetings.

After this global feasting event in Taipei, all of us now have the feeling that we absolutely cannot go back to take the old way. At this time we must stand on the foundation of the feast, and, based on the districts where they live, divide the saints up into one hundred districts. This will enhance the care for the saints and the home meetings. Moreover, we must also set a goal for the church that from now on we would establish the following four items—the habit of door-knocking, the home meetings, the meetings of mutuality, and the churches for the building up of the Body of Christ.

THE FAILURE IN THREE MATTERS IN THE PAST

The Failure in the Preaching of the Gospel

In the former way, the old way, we completely failed in three matters. The first matter was the preaching of the gospel. The churches in the Lord's recovery are not the only ones who have failed in this matter. During the past twenty years, the number of Christians in Christianity and its various denominations in the world has also been declining. This shows us that all the Christian groups are facing the same problem of a lack of impact in the preaching of the gospel. We all must study to find out how to deal with this decrease in number. Consider ourselves for example. During the last ten years what has troubled me the most is the lack of increase in numbers. I have observed the churches in Taiwan and the churches in Southern California, and they are the same. For example, the eight churches surrounding Anaheim had over one thousand people ten years ago, but today, ten years later, the number has not increased and is even below one thousand. The number of saints in the church in Taipei is also decreasing, not increasing. This shows that although the preaching of the gospel in the old way has had a little effect, it has not been successful in keeping and gaining people.

The Failure in the Home Meetings

The second item that we have failed in is the home meetings. The Bible says explicitly that the saints were in the temple and were breaking bread from house to house (Acts 2:46). Every day in the temple and from house to house they announced the gospel of Jesus as the Christ (5:42). As a result of the feast, all the saints now have home meetings. However, while those in the various denominations in Protestantism have taken the lead to fail in this matter, we have also been very short in this matter. Hence, in October of 1984 I came back to Taipei and released a series of messages on the propagation and increase of the church. In the first message I mentioned that home meetings are the basis of the building up of the church. I hope that we all would have a new start after this failure.

The Failure in Speaking

The third item that we have failed in is speaking. First Corinthians 14 says that when the whole church comes together in one place, each one has a psalm, a teaching, a revelation, a tongue, or an interpretation (vv. 23, 26). Here it says that "each one has," showing that according to the Bible, church meetings should not be meetings in which one person speaks and everyone else listens but meetings in which everyone speaks for the Lord. Brother Nee told us that church meetings should be full of mutuality. The meetings according to the Bible are not one-sided but mutual, full of everyone speaking and listening to one another. Hence, a proper church meeting should be full of mutuality. Hebrews 10:25 says, "Not abandoning our own assembling together...but exhorting one another." This verse clearly shows us that a proper church meeting is for everyone because such a meeting is mutual. The Bible does not say that there has to be a message meeting on Lord's Day morning. Rather, it says that there has to be mutual speaking and listening in the meetings of the church. We have not carried out what the Bible shows us. This is our failure.

OUR WAY OF WORKING
NEEDING TO BE IMPROVED CONTINUALLY

In the past our gospel preaching did not have impact, our home meetings were not successful, and our meetings did not have the mutual speaking for the Lord. Our failure in these three matters prevented us from propagating and spreading and caused us to remain in a lukewarm condition. We must see that the old system does not have any retaining value and that we have to rise up to take the biblical way. Everything is difficult at the beginning, but as long as we have a start, it is not too late. Once we start taking this way, we will surely make progress quickly.

When I went to America in 1961, I had to speak in English, and every time I saw the names of people and places in America, I had trouble pronouncing them. Therefore, I bought the best English dictionary and familiarized myself with the names of people and the places where I was going to speak so that when I spoke, it would be much easier. It is not easy to change a person's accent, concept, and method, but sticking to the old way is a kind of falling backward, so I knew that I had to change myself. If I had not been willing to receive the burden to start the work in America because I was afraid of changing my accent and method, the Lord's recovery would have been limited to the Far East among the Chinese-speaking ones, and the Lord's recovery would not have reached America, Africa, Europe, and Australia.

The way we work must be advancing all the time. Without advancing, we will stick to the old way and will remain poor; however, if we are willing to make progress and to change our method, we will be rich. In truth, sticking to the old way issues in slothfulness. It would be very easy for me to release messages in Chinese in America, but in order to speak in English in a way that everyone can understand, I must aggressively look up every single important word and practice speaking it. The effort required to look up words in the dictionary, to read, to memorize, and to study is called diligence. We all must realize that for us to serve the Lord, we cannot follow a routine, stick to the old way, or enjoy ease and comfort. Rather, to serve the Lord we must be prepared in everything and force ourselves to improve. Then the Lord will have the way.

THE GOAL OF ADVANCING IN THE CHURCHES

Establishing a Habit of Preaching the Gospel by Door-knocking

Regarding establishing a habit of preaching the gospel, we are not saying that every saint has to go door-knocking. For example, even though all the people in a country are responsible for protecting their country, in practicality, those who are old, small, sick, or weak cannot be soldiers. Only those who are young and strong can bear the responsibility to protect the country. It is the same with door-knocking. This kind of gospel preaching is not according to our natural method but according to the leading of the training, which is particular and requires the paying of a price.

When we go out door-knocking, we often encounter many unpleasant faces, and it is a common thing for people to slam their doors in our face. Sometimes we may knock on hundreds of doors without getting anyone saved and baptized. Hence, when we go out door-knocking, we need patience and a meek spirit. Even when people belittle us, we should smile at them. This is the spirit we should have when preaching the gospel. The method in the old way was to invite people to the meeting hall, but the spirit of the new way is to deliver the gospel to people's homes. This way has a compelling flavor and is also very scriptural.

In Luke 14 the Lord Jesus said, "A certain man was making a great dinner and invited many; and he sent his slave at the dinner hour to say to those who had been invited, Come, for all things are now ready. And they all with one consent began to make excuses....Then the master of the house became angry and told his slave, Go out quickly into the streets and lanes of the city, and bring in here the poor and crippled and blind and lame." Later, there was still room, so the master said to the slave, "Go out into the roads and hedges and compel them to come in" (vv. 16-23). This is the same with door-knocking—we must compel people to come in.

If we do not have a spirit to compel people, we cannot go door-knocking. Everyone who goes door-knocking not only has to pay a price but also must learn the lesson that even if someone were to reproach you, you still must gladly receive him. If he still scolds you a few months later when you go to see him again, then you will have to go a third time. In the end he will be saved because there is something in man that is created by God. If we deliver the gospel to a person again and again, eventually he will be touched.

The principle of door-knocking is to begin from "Jerusalem" and then to go to "all Judea and Samaria and unto the uttermost part of the earth" (Acts 1:8), that is, from near to far, from the center to the circumference. We first have to knock on the doors of our friends and relatives, then the doors of our neighbors, and then those of the community. To do this requires us to pay a price and to have patience. Not everyone who meets in our meetings can do this. I hope that among those who meet regularly in all the churches, at least one-fourth would participate in door-knocking and would build up a habit of preaching the gospel by door-knocking. In each locality, from the beginning of the year to the end, at least one-fourth of the saints should go out door-knocking. This is the secret of the blessing on the church. Those who are aged and are restricted in their movement can support the door-knockers at home by prayer. Prayer is powerful in the activity of door-knocking.

I hope that the churches in the Lord's recovery will take the way that has been ordained by the Lord—the way of everyone preaching the gospel by door-knocking and everyone speaking for the Lord. There must be some from every church who will go door-knocking every week to deliver the name of the Lord Jesus, the Bible, and grace into every home. Even if people spit at us or kick us, we have to go again a few days later. This is the spirit of the gospel. Brother Nee once said that those who are effective in the gospel are those who have a thick face. Through regeneration our face has been thickened, and we do not care about man's reproach and opposition. With this kind of spirit, we will be able to spread the gospel to every household and even to the entire earth. At the same time, we should not care only for the present result. A person may reject us today, but after several years the Lord may raise up an environment in which this person will sense his need and will call, "O Lord Jesus." Therefore, we all have to go out according to the Lord's word into the "roads and hedges" and compel men to come. An overcoming church in the Lord's recovery must have some who have the habit of door-knocking. One-fourth of the saints should go door-knocking every week.

Establishing Meetings of Mutuality

Although we all know that everyone should speak in the meetings, in actuality there are some people who by birth truly do not know how to speak. They may be able to write but are unable to speak publicly. We should not force these ones too much. In principle everyone should speak, but practically this may not be easy to do. If in a small group meeting of ten saints, three to four saints speak in a living way, the meeting will be living. If in a meeting of twenty-five saints, six to seven speak in a living way, the meeting will also be very rich.

Establishing the Home Meetings

Moreover, we need to establish the home meetings. We first have to establish the home meetings in our own homes. This will lead us to have an overcoming living. After we wake up in the morning, we should first contact the Lord and then read two verses. This will benefit ourselves and our family as well. If every one of us practices pray-reading two verses every morning, then when we go to the meeting in the evening, we will surely have something to say, and we will spontaneously build up a habit of speaking and listening in mutuality in the meeting. Even though we may not have a set topic, it will be a rich feast because there will not be merely one dish and one flavor. Rather, there will be various items and many different flavors. Someone may speak about patience, someone else may speak about love, and someone may speak about following the spirit. If everyone exhibits Christ, the meeting will definitely be rich.

An enjoyable meeting is built up by the daily exercise of the saints. If we all build up the habit to contact the Lord and

His word once we get up in the morning, and to live in the spirit, walk according to the spirit, be burning in spirit, and live Christ throughout the day, then when we come to the meeting, we all will have something to say. In the meetings we not only can share the enlightenment and supply that we have received from the Lord's word, but we can also pray-read the hymns using our spirit. Ephesians 5:18b-19 says, "But be filled in spirit, speaking to one another in psalms and hymns and spiritual songs, singing and psalming with your heart to the Lord." Furthermore, we can also read the footnotes of the Recovery Version of the New Testament. Every footnote contains revelation, light, and supply. There are also many other spiritual publications such as the *Life-study of the Bible* and *Truth Lessons* from which we can fellowship and share.

ESTABLISHING LOCAL CHURCHES
FOR THE BUILDING UP OF THE BODY OF CHRIST

The change of system is not merely a change in outward method but a change in our being that we may be living Christians and overcomers who function in the meetings. Hence, we who have not spoken in the past now need to speak, speaking not our own words but the words of the Bible, the hymns, the life-study messages, and the *Life Lessons*. If our meetings are rich, the new ones will surely stay, and the number of saints will increase. Eventually, every saint will have a meeting in his home, and every home will be a propagation group. Then we can bring those who meet in the home meetings to the big meetings. In this way we will be building up the local churches, the Body of Christ.

CHAPTER ELEVEN

THE GOAL OF THE CHANGE IN SYSTEM AND FELLOWSHIP CONCERNING THE CAMPUS WORK

We all know that a student's purpose in studying medicine is to be a doctor, and a student's purpose in studying agriculture is to research farming techniques. Whatever a person does, he must have a goal. Three terms of the full-time training have already passed, and after these three terms of training, the trainees should know where this training is taking them and what the goal is that the training wants to achieve.

Some of you have joined the full-time training for a year, and some have joined for two years. After this period of training, some of you may go back to school, some of you may work in society, and some of you may desire to serve full-time for the rest of your lives. Regardless of where you go or what you do, you should carry out the new way according to your desire. This training is moving toward this goal, but it has not reached it to the fullest extent.

THE GOAL OF SERVING THE LORD FULL-TIME

After two thousand years Christianity has become big, old, and complicated. Its inner condition is chaotic. We saved ones must serve the Lord, and our serving the Lord must not be individualistic. Rather, we must serve in the Body. However, where in Christianity, which is so complicated, can we have the service of the Body? This is the first question. Second, what should we do on the ground of the Lord's recovery? Today to change the system is not to change our ground but to change our existing method while remaining on this ground. This mainly concerns the matter of meeting. We all admit that the condition of our meetings and the way in which we met in the past did not match the pattern in the Bible. Brother Watchman Nee even said that to have a Lord's Day message meeting is to follow the custom of the nations, that there is no need to maintain it, and that it is a kind of waste. This word is very heavy and serious.

We who serve the Lord must first see the church, and for us to see the church, we must see the ground of the church. Only when we are on the proper ground can we proceed. Second, as we stand on the proper ground, how should we serve? The most serious matter related to our service is how to meet, because all of our service hinge on the meetings. In other words, if we take the meetings away, we may say that there is almost no need for service. Consider the full-time serving ones for instance. Their service is to invite people to the meetings. They either meet with people in home meetings, invite people to small group meetings, or they themselves join the district meetings. Almost everything related to our service has to do with the meetings.

THE PURPOSE OF A CHRISTIAN MEETING

The purpose of a Christian meeting is to build up the saints individually and from this individual building to proceed to build up the church, that is, to build up the Body of Christ. Today on the whole earth, only in the Lord's recovery can we see a little building. Many Christian groups not only do not have any building, but they do not even mention the matter of building; they disregard it. This is why the Lord has not yet come back. In Matthew 16 the Lord clearly says, "Upon this rock I will build My church" (v. 18). This word has not yet been fulfilled. Today there are both many Christians and many Christian organizations on the earth, but still we cannot find any building. Even in the Lord's recovery, there is not much building. This condition is the result of meeting in an improper way.

In the past, almost sixty to eighty percent of the way we met was influenced by the traditions of Christianity. Hence, even though our meetings were different from those in the denominations, the difference was not that great. In the old and traditional meetings, it was hard to see the building. This is why we need to change the system. The change in system will enable our meetings to fulfill their function and to cause the building up of the saints and the church. We have already seen the goal of serving the Lord full-time. First, we must see the church, and second, we must see that the way and system of the service in the church is related to how we meet. Third, we must see that the meetings are for the building up of the saints and the church, the Body of Christ. Our change of the system is toward this goal.

How do we lead the saints to speak in the meetings? We need to realize that if we want a believer to speak in the meeting, he must personally have a certain kind of living as his backing and support. The old way of meeting did not require us to live an overcoming life. Even if our lives were full of failures, we still could peacefully come to the meeting every week. However, the new way of meeting requires us to be overcomers. If we are not overcomers and do not live in the spirit, we will have nothing to say in the meetings. At the most we will be able to listen to others' speaking, but we will not be able to speak to and supply others.

THE WAY TO SUPPLY PEOPLE IN THE MEETINGS

If we want to supply people through our speaking, we must be exercised in three matters. First, we must live in the spirit every moment; second, we must learn to fellowship with the Lord and experience the Lord; and third, we must enjoy the Lord and His word every day. In this way, we will inwardly and spontaneously have the word to supply and nourish others. The change of the system has just started, and what we are fellowshipping with you is a great burden that we must all receive and carry out together. If we can help all the saints to live in the spirit, fellowship with the Lord, enjoy the Lord, and enjoy His word, I believe that everyone will love to meet. Then when we come to the meetings, everyone will have both the Spirit and the word and will be able to supply others at the proper time. Recently in a meeting we saw some full-time serving saints speaking for the Lord one by one. Their speaking was full of content, full of the Spirit, and full of supply. This was very encouraging.

Many people have asked what the new way is all about. Some have answered that the new way is to preach the gospel by door-knocking. Actually, this is not true. We are changing the system and taking the new way not merely for door-knocking. For example, we have already brought thirty thousand people to salvation through door-knocking, but now we need to know how to bring these people on and how to take care of them. These are matters that are also in our study of the practice of the new way. Hence, the new way comprises not only door-knocking but also taking care of the home meetings and small group meetings. Whenever the church carries out an activity, some people like to look on with a critical eye and say vague things. Many people do not realize that the change in system to take the new way requires them to come back to meet in the Body. For them to come back to meet in the Body, they must be spiritual and overcoming.

MEETING ACCORDING TO THE SCRIPTURAL WAY TO BUILD UP THE BODY OF CHRIST

Meeting according to the scriptural way in the Lord's recovery is not for a minority of saints. Rather, a group of people must bear this burden together. Today on the earth there is at least one group of people in Taipei who speak about the Bible in the meetings. Whether they meet in big meetings or small meetings, they all have the Spirit, the word, and the supply. However, this burden is very heavy. For the saints to attain to this kind of condition in which they are able to meet in life requires them to turn to their spirit, fellowship with the Lord, and exercise to live an overcoming life. This is not an easy matter, and hundreds and thousands of people must practice this in one accord.

Today in Taipei there are around ten thousand people who meet regularly. Also, we have over thirty thousand new ones who were gained through door-knocking. But due to the lack of care, only around ten thousand of these ones are left. How can these twenty thousand people take the lead to gospelize and truthize Taiwan? This question shows us how much manpower we need in order to carry out this move. Hence, we hope that those saints who have passed through three terms of the training will seriously seek the Lord concerning whether they should serve the Lord full-time for the rest of their lives. If you decide to serve full-time, how should you proceed? First, you have to see that you must be one who knows the church and stands on the ground of the church. Second, you must work and serve according to the Bible. The biblical way of serving is to build up the saints and the church.

If we do not meet in the way of prophesying, in other words, if our meetings are not according to the Bible, then they will surely be unable to build up the saints or the church. Perhaps we may be able to bring people to salvation, but we will not be able to build them up because our meetings are not proper. Even though we may bring people to love the Lord, if we do not have the kind of meeting that is according to the Scriptures, we still will have no way to build up the Body of Christ. Today whether or not we can achieve our goal depends on whether or not we see the church, know the ground of the church, and follow the Bible absolutely. We must live out what the Bible says and take the scriptural way, especially when we meet. This requires us to be spiritual, to fellowship with the Lord, and to experience the Lord's Word. Thus, our burden is that wherever we go—whether to Taipei, Kaohsiung, South America, or even the uttermost part of the earth—this is what we would work out.

We need to be one with the ministry. The ministry is for building up the saints and building up the church, that is, the Body of Christ. This is the goal that we must see. There are over four hundred saints who want to continue serving full-time. They all have the desire to serve, have seen the church, and stand on the ground of the church. If we are not clear about the ground of the church and do not stand on the ground, we will have no way to talk about the building up of the church. If we want to talk about the church, we must have the vision of the church, and we must stand on the ground of the church. At the same time, in our service we must come back to the Bible, and we must serve according to the Bible. If our service goes against what is in the Bible, our service will not build up the saints and the church.

We need to come back to the Bible and walk according to the Bible. First, we have to meet the Lord's demand for us to live in the spirit every day, to fellowship with the Lord, to pay the price, and to be those who are filled with the Holy Spirit. This is what God wants. Second, we have to begin our work, that is, to do this work. Our work is our living. We live this kind of living because only this kind of living, this kind of work, can build up the Body of Christ, and only when the Body of Christ is built up will the Lord have the way to come back. This requires that we have the vision and that we carry it out practically.

QUESTIONS AND ANSWERS

Question: We feel that we are not skillful enough in the matter of service. Can we still carry out the change of system and take the new way?

Answer: It does not matter whether or not you are skillful. To become skillful requires experience and time. The most essential thing is that we all have to get on the right track. We hope that all the full-time serving ones and elders will get on the right track. If they do, it will not be difficult for the whole church to preach the gospel or to gain people. The reason that our gospel is not strong is that we do not have the kind of living that we mentioned earlier as our base. If we truly had that kind of living and meeting, our preaching of the gospel and gaining of people would surely be effective.

In the past our work did not have much impact because our system was wrong and because we were off, particularly in the matter of meeting. However, the Lord has given us a new start. Our home meetings, small group meetings, and districts meetings will all be brand new. At the same time, the way is very clear. Now the most important thing is that four groups of people—the elders, the co-workers, the full-timers, and the trainees—go on together. If these four groups of people do not go on and enter into the new way, it will be very difficult for the churches to go on. If these four groups of people take the lead to enter in and go on in life, then the saints will be able to follow. In practicality, the co-workers particularly need to establish this as the goal of their work.

Question: Through this fellowship, the goal of our work is getting clearer. But we want to know how we can practically cooperate with and carry out what the ministry has seen.

Answer: Even though we have not fully seen the goal, we will gradually get on the right track. This will require much effort, much prayer, and much living in the spirit. After receiving the burden, we will spontaneously apply it and exercise in the meeting. In the meetings we still may not know when we should open our mouths and when we should not, but this does not matter. For example, when you are learning how to play basketball, as long as you practice enough on the court, you will automatically learn when to pass the ball and when to shoot the ball. You simply need to play and practice, and eventually you will learn the secrets.

Today whatever secular people do, they do it with all their time and being. If they do not concentrate on doing one thing, it is very hard for them to be good at it. For instance, if a teacher does not spend all his time teaching, he will not teach well or become a famous teacher or professor. Hence, to serve the Lord full-time and have a job at the same time is almost always a hindrance and an entanglement. If the Lord has not arranged the environment for you to have a job and is allowing you to serve full-time, this is a great mercy. If I had taken a job and had not served full-time in a concentrated way every day for the past sixty years, I am afraid that I would have accomplished only one-fourth of what I have done to this day. Hence, it is very precious to be able to serve the Lord full-time.

We who serve the Lord full-time also have to practice how to work, that is, how to meet. The work that we do should be either in the small groups or in the home meetings. This is a great opportunity for us to learn how to serve properly. I hope that we all would spend time to learn how to meet properly. For example, if in a meeting of more than one hundred saints there are more than twenty who know how to meet, the meeting will definitely be rich. This depends on the full-timers. Since the rest of the saints are working, they are very busy and only have time to serve after work. They are not like the full-timers who can devote all of their energy to studying how to serve, how to pray, how to follow the spirit, and how to release the spirit. This is the difference between us and them. We have to know that truth and life are our capital. Our capital is our qualification.

Question: Because we are all serving on the college campuses, and usually our work is to contact students, we do not really have much time to go to the communities. Is this all right?

Answer: Actually, there should be some full-timers who labor in the schools and some who work in the communities. One person cannot take care of both sides.

Question: At present we have several brothers coordinating together to gather seven to eight brothers and sisters who are students leading them to pray and enter into the Lord's Word and training them how to function in the meetings. Is this proper?

Answer: This is good, but you still have to study while you are carrying out this way because it is hard to set a pattern for a certain matter in one day. You have to carry out this way personally, and as you are doing it, you have to study it and fellowship with the more experienced ones. As long as you are diligent in doing it, you will find a way. For example, if you want to go to a certain place, as long as you keep asking for directions as you go, eventually you will arrive there. But if you stay in one place asking, you will never get on the way. You should at least get on the way. You should walk and believe that as long as you continue trying, you will find the way.

The prospects of what you have fellowshipped may be very good, but it will take a period of time to work this out. Because many people have not entered into and do not understand what we are doing, they may say their own things and may even criticize us. I want you to know that these practices of the new way are divine and in the divine realm, so it will be very hard for people on the outside to understand what we are doing. If you are not in the midst of this new way and do not have a part in it, you also will not understand, because the methods of this way are not the same as those of the past. Some people may ask, "Why do we have to preach the gospel by door-knocking? If we preach the gospel without knocking on doors, does this mean that we are not preaching the gospel?" No one has said that if you do not knock on doors, you are not preaching the gospel. When you go to preach the gospel, you can do it in various ways. However, if you go out to preach the gospel, you will realize that door-knocking is the most effective way.

Those of us who are serving full-time are getting clearer in our vision, having gained more understanding in the truth and having had some growth in life. If we all have this burden within us, the Lord will surely use us. Every single thing that we do must be for the building up of the Body of Christ. Consider our old way of doing things. Can our old way of meeting build up the Body of Christ? In that kind of meeting, we even had trouble taking care of ourselves. Thus, it was impossible to have any building. Our basic system in the past was wrong. We must have a deep understanding and a clear vision regarding this.

Question: How can we enable all the saints to enter into the new way and bring their potential into full use? What we have been doing in these two to three years is, as one brother said, like beginning to learn how to walk. Based on the foundation that we have gained, how can we walk better and faster?

Answer: The church in Taipei is able to go forward, but this requires your effort—the corporate effort of the elders, the co-workers, and the full-time serving ones. I cannot encourage the working saints to take the new way too much, but as long as the elders, co-workers, and full-time brothers and sisters take this way, they will spontaneously follow, and the newly saved ones will also follow this way.

Question: Since full-timers are so important, should we lead the students under our care to join the full-time training?

Answer: I hope so. The more people that join the full-time training each year, the better.

Question: It seems very difficult to produce five hundred full-timers a year. What should we do?

Answer: If we are unable to produce five hundred full-timers, it will be good to have even two hundred. If we have two hundred or more full-timers each year, that will be quite good.

Question: If we do well, we will be able to produce more full-time serving ones, and if more new ones are brought in, there will correspondingly be more full-timers. Is this correct?

Answer: You who are the first group of full-time trainees are the pioneers. If you can break through in this matter, it will be easier for those who follow, and a great part of the situation will be set. The breakthrough must be in the meetings. We must spend much effort in the meetings so that every meeting—the district meetings, the small group meetings, and the home meetings—will be successful. This is the goal of our work as full-time serving ones. We have to see that our goal is not merely to bring people to salvation. We were unable to bring the thirty thousand people whom we brought to salvation fully into the church life because our meetings were not up-to-date. If our meetings are up-to-date, at least half of our new ones will be brought into the church life. Moreover, if there is a need on the campuses, there can also be district meetings there.

The campus work should gain at least half of the students who are saved, not merely one-fourth. For instance, for every two students who are saved, at least one of them should eventually be meeting with us. Currently there are twenty-seven brothers and sisters who are serving on the campuses. I hope that the brothers will fellowship with us more often, try what we have fellowshipped, and then some time later come back to fellowship and discuss their progress with us. In this way we will be able to help them according to their need.

Question: Can you give the young people more fellowship before you go back to America?

Answer: No doubt you are hoping that I can fellowship more with you regarding the campus work. However, I have not been to the campuses, so I do not know what the campus environment is like. If your environment does not allow you to do anything, then you should go to the communities. There are always many aspects to such matters and also to our work.

Question: You have encouraged the high schoolers to choose Taiwan Normal University as their first choice so that later they may gain people there through their preaching. I would like to ask you whether it would be better for the brothers and sisters who graduate from Normal University to go to the training for a year before they go preaching or should they go preaching to gain people right after they graduate?

Answer: As a rule, they should first be trained. It would be good for them to go through a year of the full-time training. Training forms a base that can help a person to serve the Lord for his whole life. In brief, it makes a difference whether or not a person is trained.

CHAPTER TWELVE

TAKING THE NEW WAY
BY THE CHANGE IN SYSTEM

Scripture Reading: Rev. 22:13; Phil. 1:5-6; Heb. 12:2

PRAISING HIM FOR THE PAST
AND RELYING ON HIM FOR THE FUTURE

We praise the Lord for how He has led us in these past two to three years. We praise the Lord for what He has done. We also would like to fellowship with all the saints about the Lord's work and leading among us in various aspects during these three years so that the saints will know what the Lord has done in our midst. At the same time, we also want to fellowship with the saints about our future prospects.

Stanza four of *Hymns,* #149 in the Chinese hymnal says, "Jesus, Thou art the First and the Last… / Praise Thee, Lord, for all the past; / On Thee, Lord, for the future we rely." We truly praise the Lord for the change of system in the past, and we also rely on Him for the change of system in the future. He is the Author and the Perfecter, the Alpha and the Omega, and the First and the Last.

THE PREPARATION FOR THE CHANGE IN SYSTEM

Changing the system can be likened to changing the direction of a car by turning the car's steering wheel. During the past three years, although from the very beginning we have loudly proclaimed the new way, urging others to take the new way and to change, the "steering wheel" of this "car" has not only been slow to turn but has at times even returned to its original position. In addition, sometimes while we are trying to take this way, it seems that although the engine is running, the car is not moving. We are so busy, but it seems that although there is loud thunder, there is not a drop of rain. What is the matter? Actually, the reason for this is that we have been studying, experimenting, and preparing this whole time.

In 1984 when we mentioned the change in system, we never thought that it would require so much work and so many people. Although we mentioned the change in system that year, we did not do that much. In the following year, due to the lack of formal training, we also did not do much. About eighty percent of my time was devoted to the Chinese Recovery Version of the New Testament. Hence, I could not do much related to the change in system.

TAKING THE NEW WAY
BY EXPERIMENTING AND HOLDING THE TRAINING
ACCORDING TO THE BURDEN

In 1986 we felt that in order to carry out the new way we had to have a training and that this training would serve as a laboratory for us to study and develop the way that we should take in the future. At the beginning when we changed the system, we were very clear that we had never walked on this new way and did not have enough experience, but we still tried to take this way. We were walking as we were trying to take this way, and we were studying this way while we were working it out. Thus, in 1986 we deeply felt that if we wanted to experiment, we had to have a training.

Once the training started, there were all kinds of needs. Therefore, we concentrated all of our serving manpower, material means, and financial power in Taipei. We received the burden from the Lord that from the second half of 1984 the Lord's recovery had to change its appearance and not continue in its past condition, because our way of meeting and much of our past condition was not according to the Bible. Our leading co-worker, Brother Watchman Nee, once said that our way of meeting on the Lord's Day followed the custom of the nations. He said that it was a waste and that there was no need to maintain it.

OBSERVING THE WHOLE EARTH AND CHOOSING TAIPEI TO START THE TRAINING

For a very long period of time, we observed that Taiwan was the center of the Lord's recovery in the eastern hemisphere and that the United States was the center of the Lord's recovery in the western hemisphere. We also observed that the churches in both places were not moving and that there was no increase in the number of saints. The situation was the same in both Taiwan and the United States. However, there was a reason for choosing Taiwan as the starting point of the change in system. On the positive side, no other place out of more than nine hundred localities in the six continents of the world was more suitable than Taipei to be a model in starting the change in system. So at that time we arranged to have the training center here in Taipei because the church in Taipei was qualified in every aspect to help carry out the training. The church in Taipei is big, the number of saints is great, the saints' momentum is strong, and there is a practical one accord. For this we are truly full of thanksgiving to the Lord.

GRATITUDE FOR THE HARMONIOUS COORDINATION OF ALL THE CHURCHES WITH THE TRAINING

Many who know all the processes and situations that we go through to get things done in the training have said that it is marvelous that over six hundred Americans have come to Taiwan to coordinate with over three thousand saints here in Taipei in such harmony. It may be impossible to find this anywhere else. Thank the Lord that the training and the churches are truly in harmony. If we look at the training center, we will see that the kitchen alone is marvelous. Sometimes we have over one thousand people eating at one time, and we serve both Chinese and American food. If the saints in Taipei did not cooperate together, how could the kitchen cook for so many? If the American saints did not come, how could we make American food? We all know that eating is a great matter. If we do not eat properly, we will not want to do anything or be able to do anything. In the medical office there are American doctors and Chinese doctors and also American nurses and Chinese nurses. There has not been one emergency that we were unable to handle. This kind of coordination is blended and harmonious. For this reason, we truly thank the elders, co-workers, and especially all the saints in Taipei. This has been a move for His recovery in the reality of the Body of Christ.

THE "FEAST" BLENDING THE RESULT OF THE TRAINING WITH THE CHURCHES

The past "feast" was truly a great blending for us. Before the feast we had already been considering how to blend the people whom we had brought to salvation through the door-knocking in the training with the saints meeting in the church in Taipei. We had been trying to connect them for over a year, but we still had not found a proper way before the feast. However, in late October this matter was fully accomplished in the feast. The new ones who had been saved through the training and the saints in the church were fully blended into a hundred booths (cf. Lev. 23:42). The result of the feast was that those who joined the Lord's Day meetings in various districts for the past five weeks have all testified that every district meeting caused them to worship God.

THE TRAINING CAUSING THE CHURCHES TO SUFFER TEMPORARY LOSS

In 1985 we did not see any results from our promoting of the small groups, but in February and March of 1986, the results of the small groups were manifested. According to the statistics from the church office, there were over three thousand people meeting in the small groups in March, over four thousand in April, and over five thousand in May. However, the training was a major interruption to the small groups. Our experience in the church life over several decades has shown us that when there is a training or conference, the church will suffer temporarily. Because everyone is concentrating on the training, the church meetings will naturally be neglected. For example, if a company allows some department heads to temporarily set aside their jobs to get further education, then the business of the company will surely suffer some loss. However, this loss will eventually be compensated and rewarded. This is the reason that in 1986 the number of people in the small groups exceeded five thousand, but when we began to prepare for the training in July, the small groups were neglected, and the numbers dropped.

Since the training began, there has been a need for laborers. For instance, the preparation of food in the kitchen requires much coordination. Because there were not enough laborers, the number of saints in the meetings of the church in Taipei dropped. Moreover, in the second half of the last year, an evening training was added. Many elderly saints put on their training uniforms and joined the training, so the situation of the small groups became even worse. However, we are very clear that the decline in number does not matter because it is only temporary. When everyone comes back from the training, the whole church will be happy. In a similar way, when a company sends out a group of workers to another country for further study, the business will surely suffer temporary loss. However, when they come back, the level of business will surely rise.

THE GENERAL SITUATION OF THE NUMBER OF PEOPLE IN THE CHURCH IN TAIPEI

After the feast we recovered over two thousand two hundred saints who had not been meeting for a long time and started meetings in their homes immediately. Once they began to meet, they were enlivened and started functioning. When we invited them to the meeting hall, they were not willing to come, but they were willing to meet in the homes. Consequently the number of people who meet in the church life in Taipei is a little over five thousand. Because some of them take turns coming to the meetings, the actual number in the meetings is around three thousand. During the past year and a half more than thirty thousand people have been baptized through the trainees' door-knocking. Among these thirty thousand new ones, only five thousand are being taken care of and remain due to the lack of laborers. The trainees have been laboring every day without stopping in order to take care of these five thousand people. Among these five thousand, there are a little over three thousand who have meetings in homes. Some of these meetings are small group meetings and some are bread-breaking meetings. This is the result of our door-knocking.

THE OBJECT AND GOAL OF OUR LABOR

In short, there are over five thousand saints who meet in the meeting halls, over five thousand new ones who are under our care in the communities, and two thousand two hundred saints who have been recently recovered. Thus, there are around twelve thousand saints total. Besides these, we gained one thousand seven hundred to one thousand eight hundred people through our door-knocking during the feast. This makes the total number roughly fourteen thousand. These fourteen thousand are now the object and goal of our labor. However, according to the statistics from last Lord's Day, the number of those who now come to the district meetings is close to four thousand. This means that we need to take care of fourteen thousand people, of which ten thousand need to be worked on, brought to the district meetings, and fostered to live a complete and proper church life with all the saints. This will require our corporate labor. Therefore, the majority of our energy at the present stage must be focused on shepherding and taking care of these ones. This burden is extremely heavy.

THE WAY TO MEET AFTER THE CHANGE IN SYSTEM

Having had the tabernacle meeting of the feast, we feel that now is the best time to carry out the change in system. From now on in Taipei our meetings should comprise three levels, the most basic level being the home meeting, the level above being the small group meeting, and the level at the top being the district meeting. The unit of a home meeting should be a household. A small group meeting should have from seven or eight people to a little over ten but not more than that. A district meeting should have fifty people in principle, although a meeting of forty people would also be acceptable. However, if a district meeting has about seventy to eighty people, it should be divided into two district meetings. In this way, our function will be manifested, and at the same time our caring and shepherding will be more thorough. For example, in a district of fifty people there should be at least ten who take the lead, who are responsible, and who take care of others. Ten people should be able to take care of the remaining forty in a thorough and complete way. This is our principle. There should be four groups of people in the meeting—elders, co-workers, full-timers, and trainees. Currently, the number of people in these four groups of people is about one thousand. After adding the college-age young people, this number comes to one thousand three hundred to one thousand four hundred. These categories of people make up one-fourth of the existing four to five thousand people who are meeting, and they may be considered as the pillars. We are responsible to perfect the other saints to function in the district meetings.

THE MEETINGS AFTER THE CHANGE IN SYSTEM

If we want to function in the meetings, we must be living persons. The prerequisite to functioning is that we must be living. For this reason, we have many different items and levels of preparatory work. In a mere two to three months we have raised up family propagation groups. These groups have been very useful, and many families have been revived through them. This preparation began a month and a half ago when we were helping the elderly saints, telling them that they should call "O Lord Jesus" every morning when they get up and then pray-read two verses to enjoy the Lord. This practice was greatly welcomed, and gradually, many saints adopted it and formed the propagation groups.

What is it to be a living and functioning person? A living and functioning person is one who, upon rising in the morning, calls on the Lord's name, lives before the Lord, and enters into the spirit to fellowship with the Lord. He is also one who lives and walks according to the spirit throughout the day and is led by the Lord to speak for the Lord at any time and in any place. This kind of person lives an overcoming life. If a person lives in this way throughout the day, he will surely have a desire to meet, and in the meetings he will be living, he will experience the Lord and have the Lord's presence, and he will spontaneously be full of words to speak without needing any specific preparation. Most likely, our meetings will not have a specific topic but will be comprehensive, caring for every aspect. They will be similar to a love feast, which is very rich if everyone brings a little food. Our meetings should be the same. When the saints come together, each one should have an exhortation, an encouragement, a question, or a word of consolation. Everyone can bring out what they have in the meeting. This is the kind of meeting that the Bible requires.

First Corinthians 14:26 says, "Whenever you come together, each one has a psalm, has a teaching, has a revelation, has a tongue, has an interpretation." Also Hebrews 10:25 says, "Not abandoning our own assembling together...but exhorting one another." The meetings mentioned in these two verses are meetings in mutuality in which everyone speaks. If no one speaks, how can we exhort one another? From now on, we should recover these two verses by speaking in the meetings. We must confess that the pattern and form of our meetings today are not scriptural. We have not followed the Bible, so we must have a change.

NOT SPEAKING BEING REPLACED BY SPEAKING; GIVING AND HAVING IT GIVEN TO US

Brother Nee once said that if someone regularly attends meetings in which one person speaks and everyone else listens, over a period of time this way of meeting will become a habit to him and will be hard to change. If we are going to change our habit, we need something to replace it. After three years of study, we truly have many riches that can enable us to have a change. The saints, especially those in Taipei, often do not speak, even though they are actually full of riches. Often they do not speak, but when they do speak, they speak excellently. I encourage all the saints to "sell" the "cargo" that is in them. If you receive something from your propagation group at home, then when you go to the meeting in the evening, you have to sell what is in you. Never think that you will be "sold out." The biblical principle is that if you give, it will be given to you, but if you keep, even what you have kept will be taken from you (cf. Matt. 13:12). Hence, we all have to give. Our burden is to encourage all of us to bring out what we have in the meetings.

I believe that many of us have had the experience that when we did not open our mouths in a meeting, the meeting did not seem so enjoyable to us. On the contrary, we also have had the experience that when we did open our mouths in a meeting, although the meeting may have been poor, we still felt that it was a good meeting. I myself have had this experience. If I am speechless in a meeting, no matter how good the meeting is, to me it seems cold. But once I open my mouth, no matter how bad the meeting is, I myself am set on fire. Others may or may not be edified or supplied through my speaking, but at least I am supplied. Those who speak in the meetings are the first ones to be supplied whereas those who do not speak suffer loss.

I hope the elderly saints would speak in the meetings for at least two minutes. However, do not merely say, "Hallelujah! Amen!" as in the past, because this will not supply others much. Instead, you may speak about something for two minutes like Elizabeth (Luke 1:41-45), you may speak something longer for four to five minutes like Mary (vv. 46-55), or you may speak a word with content and revelation for twenty minutes like Zachariah (vv. 67-79). You may practice all these things. It is a heart-breaking matter to see one who has been meeting among us for decades and yet has not produced or manifested any gift. If the saints are willing to practice speaking a little bit more each time they meet, in a year they will be able to speak for five minutes. In this way, the meetings will be full of flavor.

THE MEETINGS IN THE NEW WAY REQUIRING US TO BE OVERCOMING

If we quarrel with our neighbor at home and then come to the meeting in the evening, we will be unable to say "Hallelujah." Suppose, however, that someone comes to us asking for trouble, but we are inwardly enjoying the Lord and consequently do not say anything back to him and are not bothered. Instead, we thank and praise the Lord. In this way we will be overcoming and will spontaneously be living in the meetings. This kind of a meeting is a scriptural meeting, a meeting that requires us to be overcoming. What is the new way? The new way requires people to be overcoming. If you are not overcoming, you will not be able to take the new way. If you do not take the new way, you will not be overcoming. From this we see that there can be no pretense in taking the new way. You cannot perform like an animal in a circus. What is the change in system? In brief, the change in system is a change in our way of meeting, and it requires everyone to be overcoming.

The new way requires us to live in our spirit. If we do not live in our spirit, we will be unable to speak in the meetings. One who lives in the spirit does not want to argue or gossip. Rather, he wants to speak the Lord's word to people, to preach the gospel, and to edify them. This kind of person will spontaneously be living and joyful when he comes to the meetings. Hence, the meetings in the new way require people to be overcoming. In the past we may have come to the kind of meeting in which one person spoke and everyone else listened, and it did not matter whether we had been overcoming or not because we were not required to speak. However, the meetings today not only require that we refrain from playing mah-jongg and from arguing, but on the positive side, they also require that we walk by the spirit, live according to the spirit, be burning in spirit, and live Christ throughout the day. If this is not the case, when we come to the meetings, we surely will have nothing to say. The meetings in the new system require us to be overcoming and to live an overcoming life. Once we are overcoming, it will not be a problem for us to preach the gospel or to do anything else.

A FURTHER WORD CONCERNING DOOR-KNOCKING AND THE NUMBER OF SAINTS WHO CAN PARTICIPATE

The most effective way to preach the gospel is through door-knocking. There is no other way that allows the gospel to be spread so widely as door-knocking. However, we know that because of the actual situations, human conditions, and the age and physical health of the saints, not all of them can go door-knocking. In a similar way, not everyone in a household can serve in the army. Door-knocking may sound quite easy, but it is not easy for us to do. It requires us to pay the price and to not care about our face. When people scold us, we still have to smile at them, and when they slam the door on us, we still have to say good-bye to them. This is not a simple matter. Therefore, our estimation is that it is sufficient for twenty-five out of a hundred saints in a meeting to go door-knocking.

I hope that all the churches would maintain this figure. From the beginning to the end of the year, one-fourth of the saints should go out door-knocking. Whoever wants to go door-knocking should go, and whoever does not want to go should not go, but he should not criticize those who go. Those who go door-knocking should not despise those who do not. Just because you go door-knocking does not mean that you are wonderful. Those who do not agree with door-knocking should not oppose it. Door-knocking is for the preaching of the gospel, and there is nothing wrong with it. If a church wants to double its number, one-fourth of those who are meeting should go out door-knocking. We must establish this kind of living in the local churches. If some do not agree, we should not condemn them. If some try to persuade us not to speak about this, we still must speak about it because this is the burden that we have received from the Lord, and we must be accountable to the Lord.

The Bible records that after man's fall God came to knock on man's "door." God came to the garden of Eden to find Adam and said, "Where are you?" (Gen. 3:9). This is door-knocking. The Triune God came to man. He did not sit in heaven and blow a trumpet, saying that He was seeking Adam, but He came to Adam. God not only knocked on Adam's "door," but He even was incarnated to become a man. While He was a man, He particularly went to a cursed city, Jericho, to visit a tax collector, a sinner who twisted the law in order to obtain bribes. It was not Zaccheus the tax collector who found the Lord Jesus, but it was the Lord Jesus who went to the tax collector (Luke 19:1-10). Moreover, the Lord also went to Samaria for a sinful woman (John 4:1-26). On that day after He found her, many more believed in the Lord (vv. 39, 41). The Lord also sent out His seventy disciples to people's houses, saying that peace would rest upon the sons of peace who deserved it (Luke 10:1-6).

In the Bible the Lord Jesus not only visited people by Himself, but He also sent out His twelve disciples, and then the seventy, two by two. I believe that those who were sent by the Lord Jesus were not elderly ones in their seventies or eighties but young people who were in their twenties or thirties. Therefore, we do not say that every saint in the meeting has to go door-knocking. Only one-fourth of those who are meeting should go door-knocking. If we apply this principle, in less than twenty years almost every door in the whole world will have been knocked on. I hope that all the churches will build up this habit of preaching the gospel by door-knocking. If you cannot do it, do not force yourself to do it, but I also ask you not to oppose it or pour cold water on it. Rather, I ask you to bring this matter to the Lord in prayer, and pray for those who go door-knocking.

THE PRINCIPLE OF OUR FUTURE EFFORT

Our meetings should include home meetings, small group meetings, and district meetings. Every morning in the homes the husband and wife should practice to have a family propagation group by pray-reading two verses. Then the whole family will be blessed. If we have this kind of living, when we bring a person to salvation, we will immediately lead him to have a home meeting and help him to establish a family propagation group. Then we may combine three to four neighboring families to have a small group meeting. Furthermore, we will have to arrange, according to the actual situation, environment, and time, to have a more important meeting on the Lord's Day as our district meeting. We should take fifty people as the standard number of people for this meeting. If there are too many people, then we should divide into two districts. In this way everyone will be able to function, and at the same time, the care will also be more thorough.

We have to do our best, starting with the foundation. We should start with the family propagation groups in the home meetings, enjoying the Lord every day, fellowshipping with the Lord, and living an overcoming life. After the home meetings are raised up, then we should labor on the small group meetings. We do not have to plan to speak or listen, but we should simply go to the meeting. If we are those who live in the Lord, we surely will be able to speak when we have to speak, sing when we have to sing, and read when we have to read. The next meeting is the district meeting. If there are fifty people, there must be ten who are more able to serve, and these ones should speak. But those who do not usually speak should not think that since there are speaking ones already, they can continue to not speak. Never think this way. You should try your best to speak for the Lord. If you speak, I speak, and everyone speaks, we will give thanks to the Lord.

All the trainees should particularly be aware that when they speak, they should not put on airs or have a superior attitude because they are someone from the training center. Rather, they should speak in a spontaneous way and in a way that is comfortable to those who are listening. I believe that the saints are willing to take this word and are clear that what we are doing today is a great thing for the Lord's sake. If this matter can be carried out among us, then the overseas churches will be able to follow.

THE CHANGE IN SYSTEM
STARTING FROM OUR PERSONAL REVIVAL

We are doing this not because our work did not have the way to proceed or because we needed to change the outward look of our work and begin anew to change the system. Actually, our work has been very much blessed by the Lord throughout the years. However, our way of meeting was not scriptural. This has been a big loss for us, and this is something that we owe the Lord. This is why we are changing our meetings. If we are not willing to take this way, the Lord will suffer a great loss, and we ourselves will suffer a great loss. Our family, the gospel, and the church will all suffer loss. For this reason, we all have to rise up and endeavor to take this new way. Whether we are participating in the home meetings, the small group meetings, or the district meetings, we have to start from ourselves—we must be those who are revived. It is not difficult to be revived. As long as we kneel down before the Lord every day, call on Him, come near to Him, enjoy His word, and live and walk in the spirit, this will be sufficient.

CHAPTER THIRTEEN

KNOWING GOD'S NEW TESTAMENT ECONOMY

Scripture Reading: Eph. 3:8-10

The deepest verses in the entire Bible are Ephesians 3:8-10, which say, "To me, less than the least of all saints, was this grace given to announce to the Gentiles the unsearchable riches of Christ as the gospel and to enlighten all that they may see what the economy of the mystery is, which throughout the ages has been hidden in God, who created all things, in order that now to the rulers and the authorities in the heavenlies the multifarious wisdom of God might be made known through the church." These verses speak of something that unbelievers cannot understand. Even those who have been Christians for years may not understand what these verses speak of because the content of these three verses is extraordinary and cannot be found in the mind and concept of man.

It has been more than one hundred years since Christianity was first preached in the East, and since the middle decades of the nineteenth century, Christianity has been quite influential in China. Sadly, however, the preaching and concepts of Christianity are too superficial and natural and are altogether according to the human concept. They have even unknowingly mingled human culture, religion, and philosophy with the teachings of the Bible. The fact is that although what man says about the Bible is superficial, the revelation of the Bible itself is not superficial; the revelation of the Bible is very mysterious. We can use the human body as an illustration. Outwardly speaking, the human body seems to be quite simple, but inwardly it is very complicated and mysterious. The Bible is the same way. Apparently it is very simple, but actually it is very mysterious.

When the Western missionaries came to preach the gospel in China, because they knew a little Chinese, they put Chinese ethics together with the Bible, telling people that the Bible also says that we should honor our parents and other ethical matters. Although honoring our parents is in the Bible, this is not the central revelation of the Bible. This can be considered to be the "skin" and "feathers" of the Bible and is neither the main point nor the crucial point.

GOD'S NEW TESTAMENT ECONOMY

The most important items in the Bible related to our human life and God's mystery are the many great and precious items that are spoken of in Ephesians 3:8-10. These verses mention three items that we must fellowship about. The first item is God's New Testament economy. Verse 9 says, "And to enlighten all that they may see what the economy of the mystery is, which throughout the ages has been hidden in God, who created all things." In eternity past, before the heavens, the earth, and all things were created, there was a mystery hidden in God that even the angels did not know. God created man in time, and from Adam to Abraham, from Abraham to Moses, from Moses to David, and through the entire age of the Old Testament, God did not allow anyone to know what this mystery was. It was only after the Lord came to the earth that this mystery was manifested.

Moreover, after the Lord's crucifixion, resurrection, and ascension, He gained a group of apostles and prophets, and through His Spirit He revealed the mystery of God to this group of people. After they received the mystery, they spoke to people about it (Eph. 3:5, 8). Among this group of people the main one was the apostle Paul. Paul wrote in his Epistles the main points of the revelation that he had received from God. As a result, this mystery is no longer a mystery to us today; it is an open revelation.

God's mystery is His hidden purpose, and this hidden purpose is to dispense Himself into His chosen people. For this He has the economy of the mystery. The word *economy* in

Chinese is quite a great word. When we say that a person is "filled with economy," we mean that when he works, he is full of plans, agendas, and methods. Ephesians 1:10 says, "Unto the economy of the fullness of the times, to head up all things in Christ, the things in the heavens and the things on the earth, in Him." God has made Christ the Head of the universe, and through all the dispensations of God and all the ages, all things will be headed up in Christ in the new heaven and new earth. This is God's eternal economy.

From the end of World War I in 1918 until now, throughout this entire seventy-year period, the whole world has been full of disturbances. The reason that the world is in a state of restless dispute is that man has denied Christ as the Head of the universe. However, the time will soon come when all things will be headed up in Christ through the church, the Body of Christ, and will be fully delivered from this state of collapse to enjoy perfect peace and harmony.

When Paul spoke about this marvelous and wonderful mystery, he did not know how to describe it, so he said, "what the economy of the mystery is" (v. 9). The Greek word for *economy* is *oikonomia,* which means "household law," implying distribution. It denotes a household management or administration, and, derivatively, a dispensation, a plan, or an economy for administration (distribution). According to the record of the Bible, God has had different dispensations in different ages. In the age of the Old Testament, God had different ways of dealing with man—He had one way in the time of Adam, another in the time of Abraham, another in the time of Moses, and still another in the time of David. In the age of the New Testament, God's dispensation toward man is to dispense Himself in Christ into His chosen people that He may gain a house to express Himself, which house is the church, the Body of Christ.

THE UNSEARCHABLE RICHES OF CHRIST

The second crucial item in the Bible is the unsearchable riches of Christ (Eph. 3:8). The riches of Christ are who He is, what He has, and what He has accomplished, attained to, and obtained for us. These riches of Christ are unsearchable and unlimited.

The Content of God's New Testament Economy

Our general understanding regarding God's salvation is that our forefather Adam sinned and fell, causing all of mankind to be trapped in sin and to become sinners before God. Although this was our condition, because of God's great love with which He loved us, He sent His only begotten Son, Jesus Christ, to accomplish redemption for us. Jesus Christ then died on the cross to deal with all of our sin, was resurrected to become the life-giving Spirit, and is now living in us to be our life. Today as long we repent, believe in Him, and receive Him as our Savior, we will be saved and regenerated, we will have the living God as our life, and we will have light, joy, and peace. Then this living God will transform us so that we may be sanctified to be like Him. This is our understanding of the salvation of God. Even though this understanding is all correct, it is not thorough enough and has not entered into the main content of God's New Testament economy.

God's eternal economy is to gain a group of people that He may dispense Himself into them to be their life and everything so that they may be joined to Him as one, be filled and occupied with Him, and be one entity with Him on the earth to be the Body of Christ, the church, for His expression. This expression begins in the church today, proceeds to the millennial kingdom in the next age, and continues in the New Jerusalem in eternity. For this, God created the universe. In this universe there is the earth, which is a globe enveloped by a layer of air, and there are various living creatures upon the earth. All these things were created for the existence of the man whom God created. Hence, man is the center of God's created universe.

Zechariah 12:1 tells us that God created the heavens, the earth, and the spirit of man. God created the heavens for the earth, the earth for man, and man with a spirit for God. God created man in three parts—the spirit in the inmost part, the soul in the inside, and the body on the outside (1 Thes. 5:23). Medical doctors study only our physical and psychological problems, which are related to our body and soul, but they do not know anything about the spirit. It is the same in education today—all the topics of study are related either to our physical or psychological needs; they totally disregard the spirit in man.

John 4:24 says, "God is Spirit, and those who worship Him must worship in spirit and truthfulness," and 2 Timothy 4:22 says, "The Lord be with your spirit." The Bible says that man has three parts. According to these two verses, the most important part is the spirit, the organ for man to contact God. This matter not only is not known by people outside of Christianity, but even many who are in Christianity do not know it. People usually confuse the spirit with the soul and are unable to distinguish between the spirit, the soul, and the heart. But in God's creation of man, He created man with three distinct parts—the outward visible part is the body, the inward invisible part is the soul, and the spirit, which is for contacting God, is enveloped within the soul. The purpose of God in creating man was to create a vessel for Himself that man would be able to receive and contain Him. This vessel within man is like a radio. A radio has an outer shell, but its most important part is its inner receiver, which enables it to receive the outward radio waves. If the receiver is broken, the radio will not work and will have no use. Because of the fall and man's sins, the spirit of the people in the world is deadened and has become like a broken radio receiver. As a result, they cannot touch or sense God and have lost their function before God.

God Becoming the All-inclusive, Life-giving Spirit

For this reason, God came to be a man, Jesus Christ. He was born of a virgin named Mary, lived on the earth for thirty-three and a half years, died on the cross to bear our sins and solve all the negative problems of the universe, was raised from the dead, and was transfigured to become the life-giving Spirit. This process may be likened to that of a grain of wheat (John 12:24). A grain of wheat is sown into the earth and dies. This death, however, is its birth. The grain of wheat passes through death and grows up out of the ground.

What is sown into the ground is one body, but what grows up out of the ground is another body (1 Cor. 15:37-44). The Lord Jesus was like a grain of wheat. What was sown into the earth was a humiliated Nazarene, but what grew up was the life-giving Spirit (v. 45).

Christ is both God and man. He both created the universe and became flesh. He also passed through human living, crucifixion, resurrection, and ascension, was made Lord and Christ, and became the life-giving Spirit. Today His divine attributes, His human virtues, and His unsearchable riches are all contained in the life-giving Spirit. This life-giving Spirit is all-inclusive, and by this Spirit, God can enter into us.

In the natural world, the best example of God entering into man is air entering into the human body. Air enters into man and has a close relationship with man's physical life. Man can survive without eating for seven days and can survive without drinking for a day, but if man does not breathe for five minutes, he will die. Hence, as far as man's physical life is concerned, eating is not as important as drinking, and drinking is not as important as breathing. Air, which is in the natural world, symbolizes the all-inclusive Spirit, who is in the spiritual world. The Spirit is the ultimate expression of the processed God. The Lord Christ is the God who created all things, became a man, passed through human living, died on the cross, and was resurrected. In resurrection He came back to His disciples in the form of the Spirit and breathed into them that they might receive the Holy Spirit (John 20:22). The Holy Spirit is the all-inclusive, life-giving Spirit whom Christ became and the breath of life who comes into us to be our life.

Today the Spirit has been completed. As long as a person confesses that Jesus is Lord, believes in Him, and opens himself to call on His name, the Spirit will immediately enter into him, causing him to be regenerated and to receive the life of God. The spirit of an unsaved sinner is deadened. But if he hears the gospel, believes that Jesus Christ is God who became a man, died for him on the cross, was resurrected, and became the life-giving Spirit, and also confesses with his mouth and calls on the Lord from deep within, saying, "O Lord Jesus," at that very moment, the Lord as the life-giving Spirit will enter into his spirit to enliven and regenerate him. To be regenerated is to receive God's life in addition to our human life. Once this person receives God's life, this life will begin to function in him so that he may be sanctified and gradually transformed. This is the way in which Christ is rich to all who call upon Him (Rom. 10:12).

THE BODY OF CHRIST—THE CHURCH

The third important item in the Bible is the church, the Body of Christ. Ephesians 3:10 says, "In order that now to the rulers and the authorities in the heavenlies the multifarious wisdom of God might be made known through the church." The church is produced from the unsearchable riches of Christ. When God's chosen people partake of and enjoy the riches of Christ, these riches constitute them into the church. Through the church, the angels—the rulers and authorities in the heavenlies—may know the multifarious wisdom of God.

We who are saved and regenerated all have this kind of wonderful opportunity. When we who have the life of God gather together and call on the Lord, the Body of Christ will have a practical expression among us and will become a testimony of God in the universe. God in His economy has to obtain this Body, not only that He may be lived out and be testified among the human race on the earth, but also that the angels may know the multifarious wisdom of God.

All of us were damaged by Satan, and all of us are fallen, have sinned, and were corrupted to the point that we were dead. But because of Christ's redemption, the Triune God came to save us. Now we are not only regenerated but are being sanctified and transformed to become a corporate person—the Body of Christ, the church. This corporate person will be His testimony on earth among men and a declaration to the heavenlies that will cause all the opposing and rebellious angels to be speechless, to prostrate themselves, and to confess the multifarious wisdom of God.

I hope we all can keep these three matters in mind—God's New Testament economy, the unsearchable riches of Christ, and the Body of Christ, the church. The reason why I fellowship with you regarding these things is that even though Christianity has been on the earth for almost two thousand years, very few people know and release this kind of truth and light. Today not only do we need this, but the whole earth needs this. Therefore, we must know these deep truths properly, study them thoroughly, dive into them, and speak them to people using everyday language. I hope that those among us in their twenties will practice this way. I believe that if we practice this, in less than ten years we all will be able to speak to people. We will be able to speak not only to the Chinese here but also to the people in other countries of the world, and we will not speak the superficial and low gospel, but we will be able to speak God's economy, which is mysterious and high.

I hope that this message will be a guide concerning the new way for the young people that they may know which way they should take as Christians and on which way they should pursue. I hope that we all will be able to read the Bible properly, know God's economy completely, know the economy of the mystery of God, pursue the unsearchable riches of Christ, and at the same time, enter into the church, which is produced by these riches for the expression of the multifarious wisdom of God. May God bless us to pursue this way from our youth that we would be those who are blessed in God's New Testament economy.

Chapter Fourteen

FELLOWSHIP WITH THE ELDERLY SAINTS CONCERNING THE BURDEN OF THE NEW WAY

When we spend more time on the young people, this can easily create a situation in the church life in which people may think that we do not pay attention to the elderly ones. However, the fact is that the elderly saints are the most precious ones in the church life. If there are not that many elderly saints in a church, that church will surely give people a feeling that there is a lack, but if there is an adequate number of elderly saints in a church, people will feel that that church is weighty. Of course, if a local church were composed of all elderly saints, that would cause us to be downhearted. There must be some young people among the elderly saints.

THE CHANGE OF SYSTEM BEING A RECOVERY

The change of system is a recovery, even an important step of recovery. Brother Watchman Nee already clearly saw this matter fifty years ago. After he saw this matter fifty years ago, when he mentioned it again later, his word was very heavy. He said that in all of Christianity, in both Catholicism and Protestantism, the Lord's Day meetings and the way of the worship of God had totally deviated from the Bible. He used a type in the Old Testament to say that they were following the customs of the nations (2 Kings 17:8). He said emphatically that this kind of Lord's Day meeting was a waste and should not be maintained. However, he also knew that it would not be easy to change because this custom is a strong tradition in Christianity. He realized that this way would not be easy to overthrow unless everyone cooperated. Brother Nee also said that this custom of the nations continued to exist because there was nothing to replace it and no proper way to substitute for it. This was also true.

Therefore, at that time he started to have the brothers' meetings and sisters' meetings. Regrettably, he did not succeed in establishing these meetings for the brothers and sisters. Up to today I deeply feel that this matter is something that I should do, and I have the burden to do this in my lifetime. Otherwise, I will be short before the Lord. Hence, I must grasp this opportunity to work it out. At the same time, the situation among us, both in the Far East and in the United States, has come to the point that we have no other way but to change the system.

THE NEW WAY BEING
A WAY THAT CAUSES US TO BE REVIVED

The way of meeting that is revealed in the Bible, the way that we are aggressively entering into and carefully practicing, will cause us to be genuinely revived. In the denominations and in our past way of meeting, people were required to attend the Lord's Day service but were not required to be revived. There were some responsible for singing, some for praying, and some for preaching, so those who attended the meeting did not need to do anything; they just needed to be there. If someone were to quarrel at home or even to commit a great sin, he could still go to the Lord's Day morning service and everything would be fine. There was once a brother who was a responsible one in a denomination. His dining table in his home was used for the Lord's table in the morning and then for playing mah-jongg after the meeting. From this we see that the old way of meeting does not require people to overcome or to be spiritual.

Today if we want to take the way of the recovery as revealed in the Bible, we have to be those who overcome and those who love the Lord. In other words, we must fellowship with the Lord every moment, live in the spirit every day, and walk according to the spirit. Otherwise, when we come to the meeting, we will have a meeting in which one person speaks and everyone else listens. Imagine if we are all in a meeting together, but you are down, and I am also down. In addition, some of the other saints in the meeting have just quarreled with their families at home before coming, and some others have spent the day before the meeting playing mah-jongg. If this were the case, how would we be able to function?

The scriptural way to meet is the way that God has ordained, and this God-ordained way requires us to be spiritual and to overcome in our living. In the past the brother who stood at the podium was in fear and trembling every Friday. He was afraid to lose his temper because he feared that if he did, he would not be spiritual or in an overcoming condition, and, as a result, he would not be able to speak on the Lord's Day. However, after he spoke the message in the Lord's Day meeting, his whole being would relax and become loose and free. The new way today, however, requires not merely one person to stand at the podium, but it requires everyone to "stand at the podium." Everyone has to function in the meeting. At the very least, everyone has to pray. If we quarrel with our family and throw our chopsticks during dinner, when we come to the meeting, not only will we be unable to say anything, but we will not even be able to call "O Lord." We all have had this kind of experience. Sometimes we do not even have the boldness to come to the meeting. This is our situation.

The kind of meeting that is revealed in the Bible is one in which everyone functions by praying, singing, speaking, and testifying. To be able to do these things requires us to live in the spirit. We must be those who love the Lord, who are consecrated to Him, who fellowship with Him, and who walk according to the spirit. If we are touched in our conscience that we have offended someone, we should confess it to the Lord immediately, and we should also confess it to the one whom we offended and make reconciliation with him. Only then can we recover the fellowship and be able to function in the meetings. Thus, we can see that the biblical way to meet is a way that requires us to be revived.

DOOR-KNOCKING BEING
THE BEST WAY TO PREACH THE GOSPEL

Some people have asked why we should preach the gospel

through door-knocking and where the Bible mentions door-knocking. Strictly speaking, all the visitations that took place in the Bible are examples of door-knocking. There are several examples of visitation in the Bible. In the book of Genesis, after the fall of Adam, God came to visit man personally. God called Adam and said to him, "Where are you?" (3:8-9). This was God's personal visitation to fallen Adam. God did not give Adam a command from the throne to tell Adam to repent and confess; rather, He visited Adam personally.

Approximately two thousand years ago God Himself became flesh. In so doing, He came to earth from heaven and not only visited man but also entered into man. God became a man to live together with men. The Bible does not record much of what He did on earth for the first thirty years of His life, but after He came out for His ministry, we see that He was always visiting people. He did not hold big conferences or stay in one place and ask people to come to Him. Instead, He went out, leaving His own dwelling place and visiting people in many places. He personally visited Zaccheus, a chief tax collector and sinner, and it was for this specific reason that He went to the cursed city of Jericho (Luke 19:1-10). He also personally went to Samaria to visit a thirsty woman (John 4:3-26). In addition to visiting people Himself, He also sent forth His twelve disciples to visit people (Matt. 10:5). Later, He also sent out seventy people to visit people's homes and bring them peace (Luke 10:1, 5). If there were no sons of peace in a house, the peace would return upon them (v. 6). He also told these ones that no matter which house they entered, they should remain in that house (v. 7). From this we can see that the Lord not only visited people but also even remained with them.

When the trainees recently went out to visit people, even though some people rejected them, the majority of people did open their doors to them. When people opened their doors, the trainees were able to discern who the sons of peace would be. The Lord Jesus also said that He sent us out as lambs in the midst of wolves. This indicates that in the midst of wolves, there are sheep that have been chosen by God (v. 3). Our experience of door-knocking also confirms that there are some wonderful wolves—ones who initially appear to be wolves but are actually sons of peace. Some of the sons of peace seemed to have been ready for a long time and did not need for us to speak much. Some of them even had prepared a snack for our visit.

The whole life of Paul was a life of visiting people. When he arrived at Philippi, he went to the riverside because he knew that people would be gathered there. He not only visited the people there, but he also spoke to them (Acts 16:13). Paul always grasped the opportunity to visit and supply people. Almost all of his gospel preaching was carried out by visiting people. He did not ask people to come to him; rather, almost every time he preached the gospel, he went to people.

In 1984 I went back to Taiwan and saw that the situation in Taiwan was the same as that in the United States. The situation was that there were very few newly saved ones. At that time everyone said that they did not have anyone to visit because there were not that many who had been recently saved. However, today we have almost five thousand who meet regularly on the Lord's Day. Moreover, there are over thirty thousand who were baptized through door-knocking in the communities. From these thirty thousand people, we have gained more than five thousand. This shows us that door-knocking is a very effective way to preach the gospel. Due to an insufficient number of laborers, we cannot visit all these ones, but even though this is the case, we still have to take care of them. We have their addresses and telephone numbers, so we all have to bear this heavy burden to care for these ones together.

THE NEED FOR CARE

Those who meet regularly in the meeting hall plus those who have been brought in through the door-knocking in the communities are exactly 10,000. During the feast, we also revived more than 2,200 saints who had not been meeting for a long time. From this perspective, we can see that there are 5,000 in the communities, 5,000 in the meeting hall, and 2,200 backslidden ones—a total of 12,200 who require our daily care. Furthermore, there are more than 600 high school young people and more than 500 to 600 junior high young people, totaling around 14,000. All these people are here, and we need to care for them.

Among the 2,200 recovered ones, most of them are willing to have small group meetings with those in their neighborhood. They are able to do this, but they are not able to come to other meetings. They like to meet in people's homes or to pick up the responsibility to meet in their own homes, but they are not willing to come to meet at the meeting hall. Of the 5,000 who were gained from door-knocking, less than 1,000 are willing to meet in the meeting hall. Among these ones, less than 1,000 are presently willing to have small group meetings, but this number is gradually increasing. The trainees have been taught that after they baptize someone, they should immediately establish a home meeting in his home and then blend the new ones together and establish a small group meeting with three to five families. Thus, the need for the care of the home meetings and small group meetings is more and more desperate.

THE FUNCTIONS OF THE ELDERLY SAINTS IN THE NEW WAY

Following in Their Spirit

According to our observation, the first function of the elderly saints is that they must follow in their spirit. In addition, they must also follow in their prayers and in their care.

Coordinating with the Young People and Making Up Their Lack

There is also a practical need concerning the trainees that can be met by the elderly saints. Most of the trainees are around twenty-five years of age. Even though they are willing to pay the price to learn, they are still young. Among those whom they have gained through door-knocking, there are some who are successful and famous. Some of the ones whom they have gained are professors or businessmen who are in their middle age. They may be forty, fifty, or even sixty years old. Although the young people surprised them when they knocked on their doors and spoke something to them that convinced them, after the young people baptize these ones, they are not able to lead them on. The young people are unable to handle their problems regarding their family, finances, marriage, and children. If the elderly saints coordinate with the young people and occasionally go out with them, not every day but maybe once a week, accompanying the young people to visit the new ones in their homes, when the new ones raise questions related to human life, the elderly saints will be able to render help to them simply by speaking three to five sentences. At present, this is a desperate need.

According to the report from the training center, the 30,000 baptized ones whom we gained through door-knocking in the communities came from knocking on the doors of over 60,000 households. These families have a very good impression of us. The trainees are taking care of them and have built up a very good relationship with them. Thus, on the one hand, if we send the trainees away, we will miss many people; on the other hand, these young trainees are not able to meet all the needs. Hence, the elderly saints have to accompany them. They need only to speak a few sentences at crucial junctures, and by doing this the young ones will receive the needed help. In the church if the elderly saints coordinate with the younger saints and completely blend with them as one, this will give people a very good impression and will cause them to respect us, envy us, and sense that God is truly in our midst.

Taking Care of the Students

The church also has to spend some effort to bring in students. If students are to be brought in, however, they need more care than anyone else. Many college students are from the middle or the southern part of Taiwan. They have left their homes and have come alone to study in Taipei. If we can bring these students in, the elderly saints will be able to contact them in the meetings and invite them to their homes for meals so that the students can enjoy the warmth and taste of the family. This will be more helpful than speaking several messages to them. Moreover, some of these students may be weak physically, may have done something wrong, or may have encountered some frustrations. If the elderly saints take care of them, comfort them like fathers and mothers, and express the warmth of the church to them, these students surely will remain in the church life. All these aspects of caring for them are not easy for the young people to undertake.

Furthermore, in the work with the students, matters related to marriage and making friends require the teaching and protection of the elderly saints. Today Taiwan is the same as America. Young males and females require proper protection and enlightening from parents. Now there are so many of these young students who have been baptized and are coming into the church. These ones really need the elderly saints to enlighten them and care for them like their parents. Most of the young people who come to study or work in factories are like children wandering around, without being properly cared for. It is not enough for them merely to come to a meeting. The elderly saints need to open their homes to receive them and care for them.

COMING BACK TO THE PROPER WAY
TO MEET AND SERVE IN THE SCRIPTURES

Three years ago we felt that it was necessary for the Lord's recovery to change the system. After much careful consideration and study, we felt that there was no other place more proper and suitable to start to do this than Taipei, Taiwan. The church in Taipei is a stable church and has been here for many years. Many elderly saints are here and have remained stable over the years. This stability is the capital of Taipei. Therefore, in these years we have not labored in other places, but we have labored specifically in Taipei. We hope that we will be able to work out a model here in three to five years, then we will help the churches in other regions.

The saints in Taipei are gradually getting clear that we are being trained to bring us back to the proper way to meet and serve according to the Bible. We are all getting older in years, and the success of this matter is not an effort of two or three days. However, we have already figured out the way,

prepared the "car," and have the "drivers." Now what we need
are an enduring character and a long-term endeavor that are
unshakable to the end. By the Lord's grace, we need to practice before God every day, saying, "O Lord, I love You. I desire
to have fellowship with You, to walk according to the spirit, to
live in spirit, and to be burning in spirit. O Lord, in any situation, at any time, and in any place I want to be able to speak. I
want to enjoy You in Your Word and share You with others."

If we all practice this every day with endurance, attend
every home meeting, small group meeting, and district meeting, and function in every meeting, then the new way will
definitely be successful. We may not be able to see the success
in our lifetime, but we can have the assurance that the new
way will eventually be successful. When we considered buying
land to build a big meeting hall, many people said to me,
"Brother Lee, why do you have to do this? Look at your age
and how flourishing your work is. This is already good
enough. You should relax and rest. You should just do what
you are able to do and let go of other things. Why should you
bother with buying land? You may not even be here by the
time the big meeting hall is finished. Then your effort will be
in vain." When people spoke to me in this way, I told them
that the big meeting hall is not for my use but for the use of
all the saints and all the churches. Since the Lord gave us the
burden to change the system, we believe that one day the
churches in Taiwan will have such a need.

EVERYTHING BEING FOR THE LORD'S RECOVERY

Today my labor and work on the Recovery Version of the
New Testament is the same—I am doing this work because
there is truly the need. We need a good translation that contains the supply of life and shining of light so that the saints
may freely use it. Hence, the Recovery Version of the New
Testament is not for myself but for the Lord's recovery. It
is the same with the Chinese hymnal. Before the hymnal was
reorganized in 1965, we had to bring six to seven hymnals to
the meetings. Thus, in 1966 I spent the time to reorganize all
the hymns and added two hundred new hymns. As a result,
we have over seven hundred hymns that we use today. All

these things are not merely for our generation but for all the saints in the Lord's recovery.

Many of the revelations that Brother Nee received were released, but because they were not published in written form, the majority of them were lost when Brother Nee went to be with the Lord. We do not want this to happen again. We want to do all that we can to keep the revelations that we receive while we are here on the earth to become the property of the church. Please pray for this matter and ask for the covering of the Lord's precious blood because this is merely the beginning. We are just experimenting and learning while we are doing. Hence, we cannot make everything clear at one time. Nevertheless, we must thank the Lord that the biggest part has taken shape. May the Lord continue to bring us on in this burden.